The Economic and Political Development of the Sudan

Also by Francis A. Lees

FOREIGN BANKING AND INVESTMENT IN THE UNITED STATES

INTERNATIONAL BANKING AND FINANCE

INTERNATIONAL FINANCIAL MARKETS

Also by Hugh C. Brooks

REFUGEES SOUTH OF THE SAHARA

AFRICA AND INTERNATIONAL ORGANIZATION

The Economic and Political Development of the Sudan

Francis A. Lees

and

Hugh C. Brooks

Routledge
Taylor & Francis Group
LONDON AND NEW YORK

First published 1977 by Westview Press

Published 2018 by Routledge
52 Vanderbilt Avenue, New York, NY 10017
2 Park Square, Milton Park, Abingdon, Oxon OX14 4RN

Routledge is an imprint of the Taylor & Francis Group, an informa business

Library of Congress Cataloging in Publication Data

Lees, Francis A.
The economic and political development of the Sudan.

Bibliography: p.
Includes index.
1. Sudan—Economic conditions. 2. Sudan—Economic policy. I. Brooks, Hugh C., 1922– joint author. II. Title.
HC591.S8L43 330.9'624'04 77-5252

ISBN 13: 978-0-367-02229-7 (hbk)
ISBN 13: 978-0-367-17216-9 (pbk)

To the people who are working to develop a new Sudan

Contents

List of Maps and Diagrams

List of Tables

Preface

The purpose of this volume is to focus attention on the economic and political development of the Sudan, to describe the progress and problems encountered in this development process, and to bring into a single book a comprehensive consideration of the situation in the Sudan. In terms of land area the Sudan is the largest nation in Africa, and one of the most sparsely populated countries in Africa. The Sudan enjoys a strategic location, commanding part of the Red Sea approach to the Suez Canal, and lying in close proximity to the rapidly growing Middle Eastern markets. Complementary aspects of food supply in the Sudan and the Middle East – the Sudan with its potential surplus – the Middle East with its needs – suggest a dynamic export growth pattern in the future.

Our actual research into the Sudan's development progress has more than confirmed early suspicions concerning lack of published information, data gaps and inadequacies, and outright contradictions in statistical information. Consequently, a considerable part of our work has been directed at piecing together semi-isolated fragments of data, analysing the why and how of statistical irreconcilables and ferreting out unpublished 'semi-official' information.

Given the paucity of published statistics and other information on the Sudan we are deeply indebted to the many Sudanese government officials and businessmen who were most generous with their time and knowledge during our travels through the Sudan. We would especially like to thank the following members of the Sudan government and civil service:

Sir Sid Ahmen, Ministry of Information; Ellayeb Almardi, Commissioner for Northern Darfur; Suleiman Abu Damis, Ministry of Industry and Mining; Saad Elizeirig, Director of the Department of Taxation; Modawi Eltiraifi, Ministry of Transportation and Communication; Abdez Rahman Yousif Haidoub, Assistant Commissioner of Labour Affairs, Kordofan Province;

Fathel Rhman Ibn Idris, Manager, Research Department, Custom Service; Khamal Khalifa, Director, Forestry Department; Taha Salih Shavey, Director of Customs Duties, Treasury Department; Yousef Gafaar Siragainour, Ministry of Labour; Hassn Abdel Salam Suliman, Assistant Director, Central Bureau of Statistics.

A special note of appreciation to Ambassador Mustafa El Medani, Sudanese representative to the United Nations, and Bona Malwal Madut Ring, Minister of State for Information, for making the research visits to the Sudan possible.

We also appreciate the help our academic colleagues on the faculty of the University of Khartoum gave us in sharing their knowledge of and insight on the country. Among others Drs Yusuf Fadl Hasan (Director, Asia–Africa Institute), Ahmed H. El Jack and Abdel-Rahman Taha (Department of Business Administration, University of Khartoum) should be mentioned.

We were fortunate to visit several industrial plants in the Gezira and in the Khartoum areas to study the various manufacturing processes. Especially helpful were: Mr Azaim, Manager, Blue Nile Brewery; Abdallah Aman, Financial Controller, Gezira Board; Abdulla Parum, Financial Controller, Sudan Gezira Board; Mohamed Khalifa, Manager, Sudan Textile Mill.

We are also indebted to the many staff experts at the various international organisations, most especially to Mr John Ducker, East African Division, The World Bank, who not only provided information but was also helpful with his comments concerning portions of the text. Also to Michele Guerard, Fiscal Affairs Department, International Monetary Fund; Antoinette Beguin, Chief of the Comprehensive National Employment Policies Branch, International Labour Office, Geneva.

Among the American government officials that were especially helpful were Carl Middleton, Director, Middle East and Africa, Overseas Private Investment Corporation; and Fred Gerlach, Economic Attaché, US Embassy, Khartoum.

Finally, gratitude must be expressed to Margaret Willaum and Kay Pellman, who suffered through the various drafts and typings while keeping up with their other tasks and maintaining their good spirits.

We hope that all the people who have helped us will feel that their efforts and time were worthwhile and that the results will be of use to their departments and to others interested in the development of the modern Sudan. A large portion of the insights of this book have been derived through their help and any shortcomings must be assumed by the authors.

F.A.L.
H.C.B.

September 1976

1 Introduction

When Allah made the Sudan, Allah laughed

Geography and history have not treated the Sudan kindly. Years ago when the Turks, and later the Egyptians and the British governed the area, few of them disagreed – nor did the majority of the local inhabitants – that the Sudan was a strange place in which to live. Mostly arid, conquered by many, it is only recently that the Sudan has begun to offer a better life to its people. Today, most of its leaders are working to develop the country into a nation. How well they succeed will affect the fortunes of not only the seventeen million Sudanese but perhaps over one hundred million residents of Africa and the Middle East.

A nation is born in time and place – geography is its mother and history its father. The Sudan was really not born until the nineteenth century and even then it faced several handicaps. Only recently have its advantages begun to be realised.

Several thousand years ago the climate of the Sudan was moist and its soil fertile. Over the past five thousand years the climate has changed and the people have had to adjust to desert conditions. Water is still the key to agricultural development and while the Nile is not as important to the Sudan as it is to Egypt, most of the people depend upon it for their livelihood.

A GEOGRAPHY

The Sudan is the largest country in Africa – just under one million square miles or nearly the size of the US east of the Mississippi. Stretching more than 1200 miles from north to south, and one thousand miles east and west, the country contains many different climatic, vegetation and physical regions, and includes people from very different ways of life, religions and cultures. The task of the modern nation-builder is to utilise these resources and cultivate these regions and people for optimum development.

Located mostly in the Sahara Desert, one is apt to think of the country in terms of a vast area of sand dunes. Yet, these occur only in the extreme north-west. From its adverse terrain, man has lived throughout the area from its earliest periods. Caucasoid stock in the north has mixed with negro stock of the south. Hemitic and Semitic people have passed through and Nilotic groups have developed within the area. After the birth of Christ, most of the area was nominally Christian but after the seventh century Islam forces began their penetration of the Nile Valley. Today, the Arabic culture, language and religion dominates the entire country except for the extreme south.[1]

Physically, the country may be thought of as a huge amphitheatre opening to the north and drained by the Nile River. Most of the Nile basin is underlined by crystalline rocks. While parts of the rim are also composed of this rock, they are also the result of continental uplift and its resulting folding, faulting and volcanic activity. They have some potential for metallic minerals and already copper is being extracted. In the south of the basin the basement rock is covered by more recent deposits of sandstone and limestone. These deposits are the result of weathering under arid conditions and, in places, form alluvial deposits from the Nile River system. The nubian sandstone, which is over 1000 ft. thick in certain areas, covers about 25 per cent of the country. The sandstone is aquiferous and is helpful in conveying the water from the wetter south to the drier north where it is extracted through wells.[2]

The Nile River dominates the draining of the basin and consists of two major tributaries – the White Nile, issuing from Lake Victoria in Uganda, and the Blue Nile, flowing from Lake Tana in Ethiopia. As Lake Victoria lies astride the Equator, it receives rains the year round and hence its discharge is relatively stable in all seasons. After leaving the Lake, the river drops off the East African highlands in a series of lakes, rapids and waterfalls but, upon entering the basin, it creates a vast swamp called the Sudd (Arabic for 'obstacle'). It is estimated that about 50 per cent of the White Nile's water is lost through evaporation in the Sudd's 1000,000 sq. miles – probably the largest swamp in the world.[3] The swamp area performs an important function in that it evens out the flow of the river by acting as a reservoir, storing water in the drier months. After about 500 miles, the river is joined by the Bhar El Ghazal which drains the rim mountains of the south-west, which form the watershed between the Nile and the Congo Rivers. A short distance later it is joined by the Sabat pouring out of south-west Ethiopia where the river drops 3000 ft. within some 45 miles. The Sabat also creates a swamp – not as large as the Sudd – but stretching some 200 miles on either side of the river near the Ethiopian border. River transportation on these rivers is possible, especially during the flood months from June to December. Together these rivers form the White Nile system which contributes some 16 per cent of the Nile's water.

From Lake Tana in Ethiopia the Blue Nile winds its way through the mountains before entering the basin. The river, which in flood carries the volcanic soil of Ethiopia, deposits this soil in its valley. For centuries the Nile has brought fresh, rich soil which makes the valley so incredibly fertile. The river flows north-west, in places almost parallel to the White Nile before the two join at Khartoum. Between the two rivers, near the junction, is the famous Gezira (Arabic for 'island'). Here the government has developed what they claim is the world's largest farm – the two million-acre Gezira cotton-growing project.

The Blue Nile contributed 63 per cent of river system water in its seasonal flood. While it is perennial during peak flood periods between August and September, its volume is fifty times its low-water level.

The Atbara also flows from Ethiopian territory and joins the Nile some 200 miles north of Khartoum. While it contributes some 21 per cent of the system's water it is not as important to the Sudan as the White and Blue tributaries. After reaching even a greater flood stage than the Blue Nile, it diminishes to a series of isolated pools in the winter.

The government has developed these tributaries for irrigation and hydro-electric power. The amount of water that the Sudan can take from the Nile River system is limited to 20 million cubic metres yearly, as most of the water is reserved under international treaty for Egypt. Hence, there is a limit to the Sudan's development of farming by irrigation.

North of the junction of the White and Blue Nile at Khartoum the rivers become the Nile River proper. The Nile continues northward cutting through the nubian sandstone and limestone deposits and, in places, cuts into the crystalline rock. When this occurs, a series of rapids or cataracts result. The Nile has six cataracts – the most famous of which is at Aswan in Egypt, but four other cataracts are in the Sudan. All are barriers to transportation and have served throughout history as borders, defence positions or trading cities. Between the cataracts the river's gradient is very gentle but river transportation through the cataracts is still difficult.

The Nile basin, as its name implies, has generally little relief and its topography is relatively uniform. Khartoum is some 1200 ft. above sea level. Vast undulating clay plains cover most of the basin, giving way in equivalent portions to sand dunes. The mountainous rim, of course, has higher relief, especially in the isolated mountains of the west where Jebel Marra attains an elevation of 10,131 ft. or in the mountains near the Red Sea where Jebel Eiba attains an elevation of 7274.

B CLIMATE

While lying wholly in the tropics, the Sudan does have several distinctive climatic regions. In the northern section temperatures are high and rainfall is sparse and seasonal, while in the south rainfall is heavy and distributed throughout the year. During the northern winter the Inter-Tropical Convergent (ITC) is over the southern region, and dry northerly winds dominate almost the entire country. They bring relatively cool, dry air to all but the extreme south. This season is very pleasant with Khartoum averaging 72 degrees in December. During the northern summer the ITC moves northward to about the centre of the country and brings with it moist, southerly winds. These bring the summer rains that reach their maximum in August. In fact, much of the Sudan receives over 50 per cent of its total annual rainfall in this one month. These continental conditions dominate all but the Red Sea area where winter rains occur. As there are few climatic barriers, climatic conditions change gradually with the latitude. Associated with the rainy season, the temperatures increase during the summer with Khartoum averaging 92 degrees in June.[4]

In the extreme south rainfall is equatorial, averaging 50–60 inches annually. Some sections of the south have a short dry season in December and June. Temperatures are not excessively high, averaging about 80 degrees, but humidity tends to be high. As one progresses northward temperatures tend to increase while rainfall and humidity decrease. At Khartoum rainfall averages less than five inches while at the Egyptian border it is under one inch. Throughout most of the country, except in the south, evaporation exceeds precipitation and hence, only limited areas can be farmed.

North of Khartoum arid conditions are dominant as rainfall becomes even more scant and even more irregular. Many areas are rainless for years at a time and then a thunderstorm may drop 2, 3, or 4 inches – often causing more damage than good. These freak storms may wash out roads and railways for miles and create havoc with transportation.

Just before the rainy season and when the vegetation is at its sparsest, winds pick up the dry soil and blow it over vast areas called ‘haboobs’. This occurs over much of the land area of the Sudan. These winds are severe enough almost to block the sunlight and periodically close the international airport at Khartoum for days at a time. Generally the surface winds help to moderate the temperature, and especially at night breezes make conditions more bearable.

Overall the climatic factor is not a positive one for the Sudan. The heat can be cruel, especially in the summer months when temperatures over 100 degrees are common. Fortunately, most of the area gets summer rainfall which helps moderate the temperature and is a great help to agriculture and grazing. Lack of rainfall is a problem, especially in the central region. Variations of between 25 and 45 per cent of normal are common. This keeps large tracts of land out of rain cultivation and forces man to rely upon pastoral activity or irrigation.

Vegetation responds closely to climate and topography. Generally, as the rainfall decreases northward or the dry season gets longer, trees become sparse and grasses become dominant, forming a savannah. These grasses attain a height of five to six feet in the south but decrease in height and density as one moves northward where there is less rainfall.

In the north, where rainfall averages under five inches, the vegetation is sparse. Grasses and swamp vegetation occur in the more favoured areas, especially in the Red Sea and Nubian Mountains; while in the drier north-west ergs, living sand-dunes stretch into Egypt and Libya and the area is almost devoid of plant growth. Southward, at about 16 degrees north, the rainfall increases to over 15 inches and the landscape is covered by scattered trees, scrub woodlands and grasses. All vegetation species exhibit the ability to store water, having deep roots and losing little of their moisture through transpiration.

Above the 20-inch rainfall line grasses dominate with arcadia trees in the better watered areas. These grasses and even some of the bushes in the central Sudan are generally sweet and make good grazing for the livestock that plays such an important role in the Sudanese economy.

In the extreme south, evergreen trees form a small area of tropical forest. Here, with rainfall taking place throughout the year, trees are the dominant form of vegetation. Tropical hardwoods or tropical crops can be utilised to help the country diversify its economic base. This then is the geographic base upon which the new Sudan has to build. (See Map 1-1, p. 16.) Overall the climate is harsh; with insufficient rainfall over most of the country, and too much rainfall in the remaining sectors. Very little of the land area of the Sudan can be considered prime agricultural land. Geologically, there are some minerals and of course new ones and new deposits will be discovered; but it is unlikely that the government can look forward to a major contribution from minerals. Climatically, most of the Sudan suffers from excessive heat and low rainfall – desert or semi-arid conditions. In short, nature has not blessed the Sudan with a rich base on which to build. Nevertheless, in the past, kingdoms

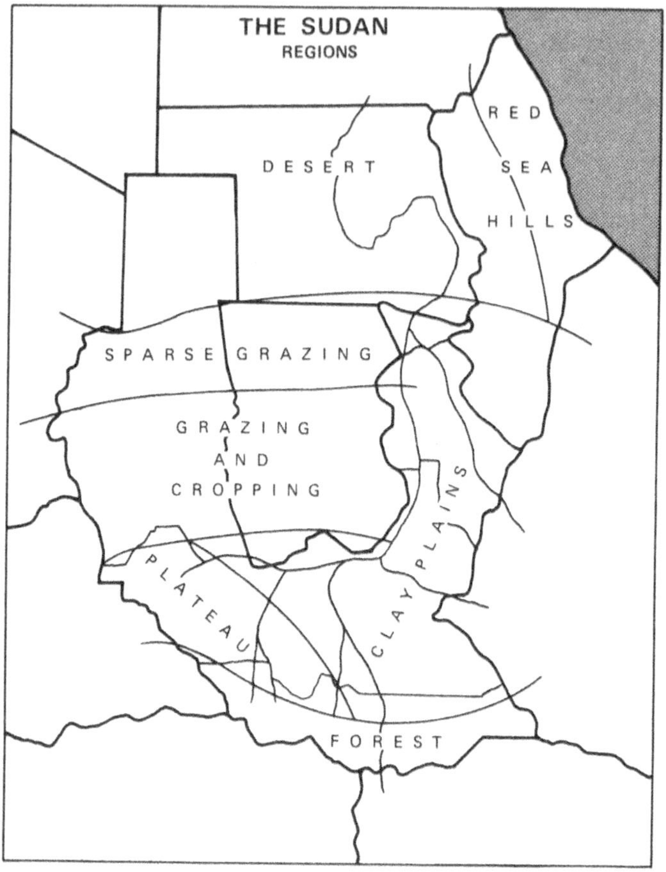

MAP 1-1

and relatively prosperous social systems have developed, lived and passed away. The Sudan's history is still being written, as is most of Africa's.

C HISTORY AND POLITICS

Most of the known early history of the Sudan is similar to Egypt's, tied to the Nile Valley area. Some 250,000 years ago early man lived near what is now Khartoum. Archaeologists have traced the Chellan culture, which gave way to the Meheulian, which in turn developed into Niholitic. These cultural stages in the evolution of man seem to have entered the area through the north via Egypt, and the Egyptian influence upon the country is a thread that one can follow throughout its history. The Sudan is a bridge between Arab North Africa and Black South Africa; but the dominant direction of influence has been from north to south. It is thought that much of the area went from grazing to agriculture; but, as climatic conditions began to change, much of it reverted back to grazing. Cattle, entering from Egypt about ten thousand years ago, provided a livelihood for man and since that time animal husbandry has played a dominant role in many parts of the country. By 5000 B.C. agriculture had developed near the river, and within a thousand years urbanisation developed near Khartoum.

As the Sudan developed it attracted the attention of its more powerful neighbour, Egypt. Time and time again armies were sent south along the river to raid, mostly for slaves and cattle. Some 2000 years B.C. the Egyptian Pharoahs built permanent forts in what is now Nubia to protect this traffic! Over the next thousand years, forts gave way to towns. Temples and pyramids were built and the Kingdom of Kush developed.[5] At one period, Kush became so powerful that it conquered Egypt and ruled it during the XXV dynasty.[6] Kush being relatively weak, it was not long until the power reverted back to Egypt and the Kush people moved their capital to Meroe, 180 miles north of Khartoum. Here iron-smelting became important, and today slag deposits testify to the size of this industry. It is thought that from this region, iron-working spread across the savannah to West Africa and down to southern Africa.

As the climate continued to deteriorate, as it has for the past 4000 years, the fragile soils became denuded and life became more and more dependent upon the river. By controlling the source of water a leader could effectively control the area. About the time of Christ the camel was introduced to the area and this 'ship of the desert' still fills a vital need in the transportation of goods and people, especially away from the Nile Valley. The Egyptians' rule was followed by Roman jurisdiction. However, Nero received reports that the country was not worth conquering so the Roman influence upon Kush was tenuous at best. The kingdom's seven-hundred-year rule ended when it was ravished from the south-east by the Kingdom of Axum in Ethiopa.

Beginning some 500 years A.D. and lasting for some 800 years, the Christians dominated life in the area. Two kingdoms in the north near Dongola and one at Soba just south of Khartoum were converted to Christianity. The two northern kingdoms especially played an important role in retarding the spread of Islam. During this period conflicts occurred periodically as the Arabs and their culture clashed with the established Christian culture. The Arabs became more powerful and the Christians, isolated from Rome or

Constantinople, gradually weakened. In 1315 Dongola fell and many tribes moved into the country and Christianity was replaced by Islam.[7] It is quite remarkable that this small kingdom kept Islam at bay after it had crossed all of North Africa and had penetrated into Spain, France and into South-east Asia as well as the gates of Vienna.

A third period of Sudanese history was the Funj Empire, established at Sennar on the Blue Nile in 1504. Its inhabitants were basically black and probably came from the west; yet the people seem to have been converted to Islam. They fought with and allied themselves with the Arabs during various periods while the Ottoman empire ruled Egypt. The Arabs infiltrated into the kingdom and dominated it not by military supremacy but by numerical and cultural superiority – yet they were subject to Funj rule. As their numbers grew in the Gezira area, they entered into a loose federation with its rulers. At its peak, the empire spread almost to the present-day borders of the Sudan. The empire fell in 1820, largely through internal strife but partially due to Egyptian intervention.[8]

Mohammed Ali won control of Egypt in 1807 by defeating the former ruling class – the Mauclukes. Some of these Mauclukes fled southward and captured Dongola in 1812. Mohammed Ali asked the Funj leaders to expel them, but because they were so largely divided among themselves they were unable to do so. Ali then sent an Army to crush them and once again Egypt was involved in Sudanese affairs. Egypt not only crushed the Dongola settlement but Ali's son continued southward to Sennar and destroyed the capital of the Funj empire.

Early Egyptian rule on the whole was probably better than indigenous rule but after Ismail Pascha, Ali's son, was killed in 1822, it disintegrated rapidly and soon revolts and massacres broke out. The Egyptians did help lay the groundwork for modern agriculture, as they introduced cotton, sugar and indigo. Under their political leadership the country also began to expand to its present borders. The Kassala area was added in 1840 and Darfur joined in 1916. Between these years, the country grew to stretch from the Red Sea to the Chad border, while its northern border with Egypt was delimited in 1899 and its southern border with Uganda in 1900. The Sudan had entered the modern era.[9]

As the country expanded Egyptian rule became weaker, and, by about 1850, began to collapse. Soon the slave trade began to grow. The first slave expedition had gone south in 1827 but met with limited success. However, by 1850 it was economically viable, and slaves and ivory began to flow northward through the Nile Valley. Not only did the trade depopulate the southern regions but it ruined indigenous economic production. It did, however, bring the matter to the attention of the world. The slavery issue and the search for the source of the Nile during the last decade of the nineteenth century once more showed the importance of the area to the world.

Samuel Baker, an Englishman, was appointed by Egypt to annex all territory in the Nile basin to suppress the slave trade and in 1870 he was made Governor of Equatorial Province in the south. Colonel (Chinese) Gordon succeeded him four years later, but neither had much success in suppressing the slave trade. Conditions were miserable not only in the south but also in the north. The civil government was oppressive and corrupt. Finally, in 1881 Mohammed Ahmed from Dongola province proclaimed himself the Mahdi and the Sudanese, weary of Egyptian misrule, flocked to his side.[10] The revolt that followed swept away most of the benefits that Mohammed Ali had introduced.

The Mahdi called for absolute acceptance of theocratic rule, creating havoc in the government, especially with the non-believers, among them almost all the southern blacks. The British, who had obtained control of Egypt in 1882 at about the time the Mahdi revolted against Egyptian rule, tried to restrain the Mahdi by using the Egyptian Army. However, the Mahdi defeated the Egyptian Army in 1883 and in 1885 even captured Khartoum and killed General Gordon. The Mahdi succeeded in completely destroying Egyptian control in the Sudan and only the port of Suakin remained in British and Egyptian control. The Mahdi's forces crossed the border into Ethiopia and at one time hoped to conquer Egypt, but they were defeated at Tushki in 1889. By 1896 British re-conquest began as Lord Kitchener fought his way up the Nile, building a railway for supplies from Wadi-Halfa as he advanced. Two years later he and the Mahdi's followers, led by Khalifa Abdallahi, clashed at the battle of Omdurman, the Khalifa's capital. Swords, spears and armour were no match for modern weapons; and during the battle the British and Egyptians lost 49 men, while some 11,000 Sudanese died. The Khalifa fled to Kordofan but a very short time later returned to the Nile Valley where he and most of his leaders were killed during a battle.

While the Mahdi and his successor the Khalifa wanted to drive the Egyptians out of the country, they succeeded only in replacing them with a stronger Anglo-Egyptian joint rule. In theory it was 'joint rule' but the Anglo-Egyptian condominium was dominated by the British. The British brought in their concepts of government, land ownership and civil service, and they also began to build an infrastructure. The railway was expanded, a dam was built at Sennar for the Gezira projects, and a college was erected at Khartoum.[11] These and other developments continued until after World War II. In this period there were ups and downs for the economy because of world economic events and British and Egyptian political events. The Sudanese Nationalists, however, continued their demands for independence and by the end of World War II had become a force to be reckoned with.[12]

The Nationalists' initial demands were independence from Egyptians. Very shortly freedom from the British was included – not that the British were better colonialists than the Egyptians, but they had a much lower profile. The Egyptians were generally in a position of dealing on a day-to-day basis with the Sudanese while the higher officials were often British. Also, many of the senior civil servants who were Egyptians left Egypt and the Sudan after the break-up of the Ottoman Empire in 1918 and went to Turkey to work, leaving a serious gap at all levels of government. These factors, plus centuries of Egyptian misrule, coloured the Nationalists' feeling towards Egypt. Periodically, even today, the Sudan expresses distrust of Egyptian policy.

While ruling the Sudan, the British soon realised that the Islamic north was much more developed than the pagan-Christian south. In a policy apparently committed to protecting autonomous developments in the south, the British forbade the use of Arabic in the three southern provinces and discouraged new Arabic settlements.[13] For a while there was talk of merging these three southern provinces with Uganda so that the Black would not be dominated by the Arab. While this plan had merit from the colonial point of view, it proved to be a major cause of serious problems that developed after independence. The plan was not officially abandoned until 1953, just prior to independence.

While Britain continued to rule the Anglo-Egyptian Sudan along with Egypt after World War II, these two countries began to diverge in policy. The prevailing pattern during this phase of the condominium was one of Britain's growing influence matched by Egypt's weakening influence. The Egyptians wanted the Sudan to become unified with Egypt, partially because of the importance of the Nile waters to Egypt. In 1951 Farouk had himself proclaimed king of Egypt and the Sudan. The Sudanese people were not in favour of this merger and wanted self-government. By 1952 Britain had agreed that the Sudan would become independent. The following year Egypt agreed to this, and the Sudan received its independence in 1956. Thus ended a period where the Sudan had the unique experience of being the only country in Africa to be at one time a colony of two countries – one English-speaking and one Arabic.

Expectations often outrun reality and independence did not bring the peace and prosperity that the country wanted. While the government rapidly 'Sudanised' the military, police and most of the Civil

Services, not all groups in the Sudan shared in this process. Many, especially in the rural areas and most particularly the southern region felt left out and discriminated against by the northerners.

Politically, the situation deteriorated; and in 1955 events came to a head when a revolt broke out and the south tried to secede.[14] For nearly seventeen years the nation was subject to internal instability by intense fighting which left the already fragile infrastructure of the southern area in ruins. A compromise was reached in 1972 that ended the conflict but reconstruction has been a slow process. Four attempted political coups, one in 1958, another in 1964 and two in 1969 – particularly due to the Anya-Nya rebellion in the south – have intensified the political instability. Two attempted coups occurred in 1976. The present government, led by Major-General Gaafar Nimeri, is trying to develop all regions of the country, both urban and rural, north and south, into a viable economic and political unit. Having learned from past experiences, the government is trying to ensure that groups like the Anya-Nya do not feel neglected or threatened and consequently resort to armed violence.

In this they have not been completely successful, as evidenced by the troubles of 1976. The government is faced with the task of uniting Africans and Arabs, with totally different religions, customs, languages and history, into a common unit.[15] The government must steer a path between extremists of both sides, as well as meet the demands of the Arab League, the Organization of African Unity, the United Nations, the developing nations, and the remnants of the Cold War. If this alone was not difficult enough, poltical intrigue by political elements in neighbouring Libya, on-going problems with the new government of Ethiopia, and age-old ties with and distrust of Egypt, compound the problem. Considering these difficulties, most observers would give the present government high marks for its internal development policies and for its non-aligned foreign policy.

The government is making use of the region's long history, which dates back to the Pharaohs of Egypt's time, to achieve nation-building objectives with traces of civilisation in the area extending back over the past 200,000 years (artifacts, pyramids, temples, forts and early urban centres have been excavated). There is much of the past to build upon. All of this history and tradition can be used to develop a sense of nationhood for the 597 individual ethnic and cultural groups that now live in the Sudan. To protect this heritage all antiquities are government property – even those found in mining operations.[16]

While the world was engaged in saving the temple at Abu-Simbel in Egypt,[17] the Sudanese took advantage of the potential flooding of a part of the Nile Valley to save some of its antiquities. Over 650 new archaeological sites were found in the Valley – along with many frescoes, tombs, and artifacts. Many of these items were removed and taken to Khartoum to form the National Museum, one of the most attractive in the world. Here they are available to all the people to see and study. This museum can be of value not only in building national and cultural pride among the local inhabitants, but also in the Sudan's quest for tourists. History is a major ingredient of tourism in Europe and the Mediterranean, and the Sudan should be able to capitalise on its rich inheritance.

Today most of the Sudanese have low incomes and standards of living. The nation is one of the poorest in the world. With proper management and some luck, however, the Sudanese should be able to utilise their potential as a food and fibre supplier to the rest of the world.[18]

2 Population and Manpower

A POPULATION

Population growth and manpower quality can be controlling variables in the economic and political development of a nation such as the Sudan. Rapid population growth places a strain on limited capital and other resources. Manpower quality influences the amount of production that can be achieved in total and *per capita*. The statistical data on population and manpower in the Sudan leave many questions unanswered. Nevertheless, the brief analysis contained in this chapter provides a perspective on the Sudan which is needed to have a balanced view of an economy in process of transition. Moreover, it introduces the researcher to some new questions concerning economic progress and manpower untilisation in the Sudan.

1 *Size and Distribution*

The first modern population census in the Sudan was conducted in 1955–6. At that time total population was estimated to be 10.3 million. The major concentrations of population were in Blue Nile Province (2069 thousand), Kordofan (1761 thousand), and Darfur Province (1328 thousand). Estimates based on the 1973 population census indicate that the total population has increased to 14.7 million. While the same three provinces contain the largest concentration of population, as eighteen years earlier, differential rates of growth are indicated (Table 2-1). For the Sudan as a whole the rate of population growth in the period 1955–73 is estimated at 2.2 per cent per annum. More recent studies by the Agency for International Development estimate population growth at 3.1 per cent per annum.

Population has grown far more rapidly in urban areas (7.4 per cent annually) as contrasted with rural areas (1.5 per cent annually). The disparity between urban and rural population growth should not be unexpected, since there has been a pronounced pattern of

TABLE 2-1 Population Growth by Province 1955–73

Province	1955–6 Census	1973 Census	Annual growth rate
Darfur	1,328,765	2,139,615	2.7
Kordofan	1,761,968	2,202,345	1.3
Khartoum	504,923	1,145,921	4.7
Blue Nile	2,069,646	3,740,405	3.2
Kassala and Red Sea	941,039	1,547,475	2.8
Northern	873,059	957,671	0.5
Equatoria	903,503	791,738	−0.7
Bahr el Gazal	991,022	1,396,913	2.0
Upper Nile	888,611	836,263	−0.4
Six northern provinces	7,479,400	11,733,432	2.7
Three southern provinces	2,783,136	3,024,914	0.5
Total	10,262,536	14,758,346	2.2

SOURCE 1955–6 Census of Population, and Department of Statistics, 1975. The 1973 census results are provisional and subject to revision.

in-migration to the provinces containing the principal urban centres (Khartoum, Blue Nile and Kassala). However, it is surprising that given the significant amount of in-migration to these centres the unemployment rate in urban centres has remained low. (See Map 2-1, p. 15.)

2 *Mobility of Population*

The population of the Sudan is mobile to a high degree. It is estimated that at least one million men and women move every year.[1] A variety of factors account for the high degree of population mobility. A high proportion of the mobile population move about from place to place in search of better income-earning opportunities. Second, Sudan has a large number of nomads who move with their cattle according to a seasonal pattern.[2] This flow runs along a north–south axis and has its largest concentration in Kassala, Darfur and Kordofan Provinces. The population census of 1955–6 indicated that the percentage of population considered nomadic in these provinces was Kassala (63 per cent), Darfur (21 per cent), and Kordofan (24 per cent). Third, there is a persistent drift of population toward urban centres, partly associated with the search for

MAP 2-1

better jobs. Fourth, there is a constant east–west flow of people through the Sudan in connection with the holy pilgrimage to Mecca. These individuals often take up temporary residence in the Sudan, sometimes for a period of several years, saving money for the next leg of the trip.

Areas that are major recipients of mobile Sudanese include the urban centres and the modern farming schemes (including the mechanised farms and irrigated agricultural areas such as the Gezira). Migration based upon opportunities for seasonal work in agriculture is of substantial magnitude. In 1973–4 the Gezira Board alone employed 542,000 people in harvesting the cotton crop, of whom 336,000 were seasonal in-migrants from other provinces.[3]

Annual migration to the mechanised farming scheme in the Nuba Mountains of southern Kordofan Province comes to 70,000 people. Similarly, in Kassala Province 100,000 migrants travel to agricultural schemes to obtain seasonal employment.

The rapid growth of urban population in the Sudan is a reflection of large gross in-migration to urban centres and towns, and a smaller amount of out-migration, partly following seasonal patterns. Data provided in the 1973 population census indicates that in the period 1955–73 urban population had grown annually at a rate of 7.4 per cent, reflecting a tripling of urban population in the Sudan.

In 1973 approximately 35 per cent of the urban population in the Sudan resided in the Three Towns area of Khartoum.[4] This reflects a growth of 6.6 per cent per annum between the taking of the 1955–6 census and the 1973 census, well over the estimated natural growth rate of population in the city of 2.5–3.0 per cent. In-migration accounts for this higher population growth rate in Khartoum. The majority of in-migrants come from Northern, Kordofan, Blue Nile and Darfur Provinces. Sample survey data indicate that the in-migrants possess better educational backgrounds than is characteristic of provincial populations from which they stem, and that these migrants tend to be relatively young. Over three-fourths of them were working in agriculture prior to migrating to Khartoum. Push and pull forces were reinforcing each other in sending migrants to Khartoum.[5] The push factors include population pressure, lack of job opportunities, lack of rain for good crops, and low incomes. Included among the pull factors are higher average annual earnings, job availability, better education, and low cost of migration due to the presence of friends and relatives (who provide shelter and basic amenities).

B MANPOWER RESOURCES AND UTILISATION

In the Sudan it is not possible to establish a precise definition and measurement of the labour force. This is due to the presence in the Sudan of a number of conditions which influence the nature of economic activity and differentiate it from economic activity as we know it in more developed countries. For example, the distinction between 'main' and 'subsidiary' activities involves a subjective judgement. In the 1955–6 census it was largely left to those enumerated to make this distinction. Another difficulty encountered in the Sudan is that many individuals do not sell their produce, but consume it themselves.[6] Therefore, they have little idea of the cash value of their income. Finally, distinctions made in the Sudan according to occupational groups conform to 'none of the available international lists of occupations . . .' and it was necessary to introduce a new list in the 1955–6 census.

1. *Labour Force and Participation Rate*

Up to the present time the only complete count of the Sudanese labour force was made in the 1955–6 census. Based on this census it was found that 46.2 per cent of the population aged five and over was engaged in a main occupation, that another 13.6 per cent was engaged in a subsidiary occupation only, and that the economically active population (sum of these two categories) was 59.8 per cent of the population aged five and over. This definition of the labour force excludes unemployed, students, and housewives.[7]

The overall participation rate of 59.8 per cent reflected in the 1955–6 census is the resultant of wide differences in labour force participation by age, sex and other characteristics. It is apparent that boys start to work at an early age, that the great majority of men are economically active, that females participate to a markedly lesser extent in economic activity, and that for females subsidiary occupations are more important by number employed than main occupations.

TABLE 2-2 Labour Force and Participation Rates (1955–6 Census Results)

	Male		*Female*		
	5–11	*Over 11*	*5–11*	*Over 11*	*Total*
	Number of persons ('000s)				
Economic activity as main occupation	692	2752	73	283	3800
Economic activity as subsidiary occupation	14	3	168	931	1116
Economically active, total	706	2754	241	1214	4915
	Participation Rate (per cent)				
Economic activity as main occupation	52.3	96.5	7.0	9.4	46.2
Economic activity as subsidiary occupation	1.1	0.1	16.0	31.1	13.6
Economically active, total	53.4	96.6	23.0	40.5	59.8

SOURCE United Nations, *Population Growth and Manpower in the Sudan*, 1964, p. 59.

Based on preliminary findings of the 1973 census, the crude participation rates of males (age 15 and over) was reported at 47.1 per cent, of females (age 15 and over) at 11.9 per cent, and the total of both sexes 29.6 per cent. It should be noted that this census employs a more restricted definition of the labour force than the earlier census, excluding most women, and all those below the age of 15 (who in fact may be working). Developing 'best guesses' of male and female participation rates defined both narrowly and broadly the ILO has come up with upper and lower estimates of the labour force in 1973 of 7.3 million and 4.7 million, an uncomfortably wide range. Clearly, one of the major tasks of labour force survey work in the Sudan over the coming years will be to develop a reasonable definition of labour force participation among men and women, and especially for women in rural households where the entire family functions as a production unit.

2 *Employment and Unemployment*

The high degree of labour mobility in the Sudan has been described. Mobility implies 'moving from job to job' and a relatively higher (frictional) unemployment level. Mechanisation of agriculture similarly suggests labour displacement on the farm and at least temporary unemployment. The high content of seasonal farm employment in the Sudan similarly suggests that seasonal unemployment may be high.

The 1955–6 census provided the only nationwide measure of unemployment until 1973. The 1955–6 census refers to a category of unemployed and beggars that represented 1.1 per cent of the labour force.[8] Adjusting for those generally active in a subsidiary occupation increases the unemployment measure to 1.7 per cent of the labour force. The 1964–6 population and housing survey and 1967–8 household budget survey found unemployment to be 3.5 per cent of the urban labour force, and 2.9 per cent of the total labour force. Provisional results of the 1973 population census yield an unemployment figure of 6.5 per cent. Moderate differences are found between urban and rural areas (5.7 per cent and 6.7 per cent respectively). However, wide differences exist between provinces. The seven northern provinces average 3.7 per cent (with a range of 2.2 per cent in Darfur to 5.2 per cent in Blue Nile). In the three southern provinces the average is 15.4 per cent. The high rates in the southern provinces reflect temporary adverse conditions persisting shortly after the termination of hostilities in that area.[9]

It is interesting to note that open unemployment rates are much lower in the Sudan than in most developing countries. With rapid growth in population in Khartoum and other urban centres the unemployment rate has remained relatively low, suggesting that the

TABLE 2-3 Occupations of Economically Active Adults: Numbers of Men and Women Reporting Main and Subsidiary Occupations in each group at the 1955/6 Census

	Adult males				*Adult females*			
	Main occupations		*Subsidiary occupations*		*Main occupations*		*Subsidiary occupations*	
Code occupational group	*number*	%	*number*	%	*number*	%	*number*	%
A. Farmers, etc.	1,868,316	67.9	300,469	44.2	222,695	78.7	730,276	77.0
J. Shepherds	279,214	10.1	113,949	16.7	7,722	2.7	7,971	0.8
B. Animal owners	150,025	5.4	108,670	16.0	1,640	0.6	7,574	0.8
8. Craftsmen, etc	79,518	2.9	54,352	8.0	20,739	7.3	152,129	16.0
F. Labourers other than farm	74,375	2.7	11,123	1.6	1,849	0.7	2,547	0.3
6. Shop owners, etc.	65,765	2.4	15,370	2.3	864	0.3	1,163	0.1
9. Skilled services	43,051	1.6	6,436	0.9	15,698	5.5	20,146	2.1
4. Semi-professional, non-technical	38,148	1.4	26,680	3.9	1,658	0.6	2,752	0.3
H. Farm labourers	37,680	1.4	29,985	4.4	3,913	1.4	20,781	2.2
D. Machinery operatives	32,663	1.2	3,772	0.6	302	0.1	511	0.1
E. Non-skilled services	29,981	1.1	2,732	0.4	2,894	1.0	1,275	0.1
C. Junior clerical, etc.	20,026	0.7	4,645	0.7	558	0.2	269	–
K. Protective services	16,899	0.6	529	0.1	30	–	221	–
5. Semi-professional, technical	6,765	0.2	283	–	2,081	0.7	641	0.1
7. Senior clerical, etc.	3,669	0.1	693	0.1	83	–	46	–
0. Professional, non-technical	2,621	0.1	290	–	236	0.1	88	–
2. Managerial	1,486	0.1	316	–	15	–	17	–
1. Professional, technical	1,108	–	25	–	21	–	25	–
3. Farm owners	196	–	124	–	39	–	2	–
All gainful occupations	2,751,506	100.0	680,443	100.0	283,037	100.0	948,434	100.0

SOURCE United Nations, *Population Growth and Manpower in the Sudan*, 1964, p. 69.

urban labour market has succeeded in absorbing increasing numbers of job seekers.

Watertight distinctions made between employed and unemployed in developed countries lend themselves only to hazy boundaries in the Sudan. Many of the unemployed work several hours a day, and it is possible to make unemployment look larger or smaller by moving the cut-off point of hours worked per day left or right along the scale. Unemployment blends into underemployment.

Underemployment tends to be reflected in the distribution of households according to income. Based on the household budget survey of 1967–8, 31 per cent of households had incomes of less than £S.100 per year. Another 43 per cent found themselves in the income bracket £S.100 to £S.200. The survey reflects an appreciable difference between urban and rural areas, as well as between provinces.

3 *Gainful Occupation*

In the report on the 1955–6 census as it pertains to occupational groups it was noted that internationally recommended classifications of economic activities were not practical. Further, it was noted that even if a classification of Sudanese manpower by international standards had been feasible,

> little would have been learned from the detailed results beyond the already known fact that Sudanese experience in specialised branches of activity and specialised types of occupation is still very limited.[10]

The general results of the occupational analysis in the 1955–6 census are summarised in Table 2-3. The results indicate that

(1) agricultural activity dominates in both main and subsidiary occupations;
(2) adult males outnumber adult females in main occupations by a ratio of 10 to 1;
(3) adult females outnumber adult males in subsidiary occupations;
(4) there is a great scarcity of professional, managerial and skilled manufacturing workers;
(5) the work force engaged in the manufacturing, commerce, and clerical categories is very small.

Data from the population census of 1973 permits a broad comparison with the findings just described. The provisional estimates (Table 2-4) indicate the following:

(1) agricultural activity continues to dominate as a source of employment, but now accounts for a somewhat lower percentage of overall employment;

(2) the scarcity of professional, managerial and skilled manufacturing workers is not as acute as eighteen years earlier;
(3) a somewhat higher percentage of the work force is engaged in the manufacturing, commerce, and clerical categories.

TABLE 2-4 Estimates of Employment by Sector and Occupation, 1973

	Percentages		
Agriculture	72.7	Professional	1.9
Manufacturing	3.7	Administrative	0.4
Electricity	1.0	Clerical	1.4
Construction	1.9	Sales	4.5
Commerce, Trade and Finance	5.2	Service	7.6
Transport	3.6	Agricultural	71.6
Services	11.9	Production	12.6
	100.0		100.0

SOURCE Population Census of 1973, provisional figures.

Additional details concerning economic activity and sectoral employment are provided from a survey of employment and earnings in establishments employing five or more employees. This survey was completed in 1973 and indicates that over 69,000 workers were employed in the public and private sectors (excluding government ministries and departments). Nearly two-thirds of these were working in manufacturing, one-sixth in wholesale-retail trade and restaurants, 10 per cent in transport and storage, approximately 5 per cent each in finance and insurance, and nearly 6 per cent in community and social services. Over 90 per cent of these workers are males. Female workers are most heavily concentrated in manufacturing (three-fourths of female workers).

C INCOME AND WAGES

Wide gaps exist in all types of statistics concerning income levels and income distribution in the Sudan. Therefore, information used in the following discussion suffers from the expected deficiencies. Data is scattered, representing the results of household surveys conducted at discrete points in time. These surveys have generally left out the southern provinces or given them inadequate representation. But even in the northern provinces the information generated does not adequately cover the more mobile elements of the population.

1 *Four Patterns of Income*

While our discussion of population has suggested that labour markets in the Sudan tend to be efficient in affording job opportunities to migrants, significant income and wage differentials persist. In the following discussion we consider four fairly distinct groups of economically active persons, each conforming to its own wage and income patterns. These four groups include urban workers employed in the modern sector, urban workers employed in the informal sector, those employed in the modern agricultural sector, and those employed in the traditional agricultural sector.

Modern sector urban labour markets in the Sudan tend to be dominated by hiring practices and wage levels of the public sector. Wage rates in the public sector are higher than in the private sector. In the public sector state enterprises such as the Sudan Railways pay better than other branches of government. Employment in modernised private industry and commerce is small in absolute amount and relative to the total labour force. Nevertheless it represents one of the highest income-earning economic activities. In a 1974 survey of households in Greater Khartoum it was found that workers enjoyed annual earnings of between £S.369 (construction) and £S.707 (finance). In between were social services (£S.458), manufacturing (£S.429), trade and hotels (£S.578), and electricity (£S.543). By occupational category unskilled workers were found to have the lowest earnings (£S.244 per annum), with professional (£S.869) and administrative (£S.1297) the highest. In between were production workers (£S.360) and clerical (£S.615).[11]

In 1974 the Minimum Wage Order adopted a figure of £S.16.50 per month (£S.3.90 weekly) as the minimum wage in the civil service and public sector enterprises. Private firms were given until 1976 to catch up to this minimum wage in three annual increments. The act applies to workers in establishments with 10 or more workers. The Minimum Wage Order of 1974 was an extremely moderate measure since public enterprises were already paying more than the minimum in 1974.

Informal sector activity refers to production of goods and services in the traditional or unmodernised way. In the past the informal sector has been viewed as unproductive or stagnant, with the implication that inefficiencies characterise the small enterprises that cluster in this sector. A different view sees the informal sector as more dynamic, and adequately serviced with creative entrepreneurial ability.[12]

The informal sector is often characterised by family ownership, small-scale output, labour-intensive production, non-technical methods, and ease of entry. In the Sudan, data on the informal sector is derived from the 1970–1 Handicraft Survey and the 1974

Household Survey. The 1974 survey indicates a total of 5300 establishments in manufacturing and repair (including 1050 in wood and furniture, 550 in motor vehicle repair, and 500 in food and beverage). In addition there are over 16,000 service and commercial establishments in the informal sector, and another 5000 transport establishments (taxis, buses, and lorries).

Earnings in the informal sector vary from one activity to another. Average daily earnings of workers in this sector have been reported at £S.0.80, equivalent to approximately £S.200 per annum. At the low end of the scale workers in footwear manufacture earn £S.0.30 per day, equivalent to £S.85 annually. Workers in electrical repair shops stand high in earnings in the informal sector with daily earnings of £S.1.24 (£S.310 per annum). These earnings figures do not refer to profits earned by proprietors, which can be quite substantial. For example, a well-established sales booth in the Arab Suq in Khartoum can earn profits of £S.2–3 daily, and a car-cleaning boy can earn £S.360 per annum.

TABLE 2-5 Four Patterns of Income in the Sudan (Annual income in £S.)

Labour force sector	*Basic range*	*Midpoint income*
Urban–Modern	300–700	500
Urban–Informal	85–310	200
Agricultural–Modern		
Owners or tenants	500–4000	2000
Workers	100–150	125
Agricultural–Traditional	20–120	70

SOURCE Authors' estimates. Data apply to 1973.

Several distinct categories of workers apply themselves in the modern agricutural sector. These include farm tenants in the irrigated areas,[13] local workers who are employed for cash wages mainly on a seasonal basis,[14] migrant workers who move about on a seasonal basis from one region to another,[15] and mechanised private farmers.[16] The mechanised farm operators can earn the highest income in the modern agricultural sector, with amounts of £S.3000–4000 per year considered average. Second highest in annual income would be the Gezira tenants who can earn £S.500–1000 per annum. Gezira cotton pickers were able to earn 50–60 piastres daily in 1974, of which two-thirds was paid in cash and the balance in food and service expenses. Assuming that these workers were employed throughout the year their annual earnings would be £S.125.

Income in the traditional agricultural sector is the lowest among the four patterns described in this section. The traditional agricultural sector embraces approximately four million workers, accounting for approximately three-fifths of those engaged in productive activity in the Sudan. These include sedentary farmers who rely on rain-fed crops in the savannah belt, Baggara cattle herders, camel herders, and migrant workers. Exchange of goods between subsistence agriculturalists is facilitated by a system of local markets where specialised traders (known as Jellaba in the western Sudan) integrate local and national economies.

In the traditional agricultural sector neither land nor labour is monetised. More important, there is a cut-off point beyond which workers value leisure higher than additional income. In cases where cash income becomes essential, cash cropping and labour migration may take place. For example, it is not uncommon for one-fifth of the male population in some villages in the lower wadis to be absent as migrant workers for periods of a month or longer.

While efforts at specifying 'average income' in the traditional sector are difficult due to lack of precise data and emphasis on non-cash income, some impressionistic generalisations are possible. Averages are deceptive due to the varied nature of economic activities pursued. For example, the cattle herder (with a herd of 200 or more animals) may have a wealth status that far exceeds that ever to expected by the urban worker with an annual income of £S.600. By comparison this same herder may pursue a most frugal existence and 'consume' less than one-tenth as much as the urban worker. In general consumption standards of the traditional farmer are less than half of those enjoyed by his urban cousin working in the modern sector. In the case of sedentary cultivators, income (mostly non-cash) may be £S.30–50 annually.

2. *Regional Comparisons*

While incomplete and suffering from statistical deficiencies, the data available on household income by province provides some interesting and useful comparisons. Data from the Household Budget Survey of 1967–8 (Table 2-6) indicates sizeable differences in average income by province. Not surprisingly, the provinces with the lowest household income are in the western Sudan (Darfur and Kordofan). These provinces are less urbanised and poorer than the eastern provinces. The most urbanised province (Khartoum) enjoys the highest household income.

The three southern provinces are not included in the above comparisons. At the time of this Survey the civil war was in its early stages. The government has adopted a policy of reducing income inequalities among the provinces, and has contributed approxi-

TABLE 2-6 Average Income of Households by Province

Province	*Average annual income (£S.)*
Northern	124
Khartoum	236
Kassala and Red Sea	183
Blue Nile	180
Kordofan	153
Darfur	98
Six provinces combined	189

SOURCE *Household Budget Survey for Sudan, 1967–68.*

mately £S.12 million per annum to the Southern Regional Fund over the period 1972–5 for this purpose. In addition budgetary deficits of the southern provinces have been defrayed by the central government.

D LABOUR LEGISLATION AND INDUSTRIAL RELATIONS

Industrial relations in the Sudan have been patterned after the British model. During the British colonial administration minimal interference was imposed by the government and legal requirements for establishing a trade union were uncomplicated and easily met.[17] A few small and relatively weak trade unions were formed, a notable exception being the Sudan Railway Workers Union (SRWU), which is the most influential of all trades unions in the nation. This trade union gained recognition from the railway company a full decade prior to the Sudan achieving political independence. In 1949 the national Workers Congress was formed as a federation of existing trade unions, and a year later this Congress became the Sudan Workers Trade Union Federation (SWTUF).

It was not until new legislation came in 1964 that the trade union movement became a significant factor in the Sudan. Following this there was substantial growth in union membership so that by 1971 there were 546 registered trade unions with a total membership of 281,607. Despite this growth in numbers, trade unions were considered in a relatively weak position. Most of the unions had a small membership (less than 200). The few large unions were confined to the public sector.

In 1967 the Sudan Employers Consultative Association was formed. This organisation is primarily concerned with labour relations but does not negotiate with trade unions on behalf of its affiliated employers. Its major activities focus on providing advisory and consultant services for its members.

During the first decade and a half of independence collective bargaining in the Sudan has played a minor and possibly even unimportant role in affecting the conditions and terms of employment in the Sudan. In the public sector conditions and terms of employment were unilaterally determined by the government. In turn, these served as a pattern for conditions and terms of employment in the private sector.

The year 1971 may be considered a dividing line in the field of labour and industrial relations in the Sudan. First, the 1949 Trade Unions Ordinance was replaced by the 1971 Trade Unions Act. This legislation restructured the trade unions into 38 blue-collar and 48 white-collar unions. These unions are structured along sectoral, industrial or occupational groupings. In 1973 the Minister of Public Service and Administration Reform produced regulations specifying the sectors in which unions might be formed. Second, the organisation of employers was restructured by the Employers Organisation Act of 1973. Following this, regulations were issued prescribing one employer organisation for each of several specific producing sectors. Third, organised labour and management have become integrated into the political mechanisms of the Sudan. The Sudan Socialist Union (SSU) has been reconstituted with five major secretariats representing farmers, workers, employers and merchants, professional employees, and the armed forces. These developments portend further changes in the institutional framework of industrial relations wherein the machinery of collective bargaining may be expected to further develop in various sectors of the economy. More significant, the new framework provides wide scope for developing a system of tripartitism between government, trade unions, and employers.

The developments described in the preceding paragraph could contribute in an important way to minimising industrial disputes in the Sudan. The Ministry of Labour is now empowered to prescribe the industrial sectors in which workers' and employers' organisations may be formed. As a result inter-union rivalry and jurisdictional disputes are not likely to cause industrial unrest. Moreover, employers are obliged to deal with recognised trade unions. In recent years strikes have been rare, in part due to a Presidential Order of 1969 which prohibits strikes. Other factors tending to minimise the likelihood of strikes in the Sudan include integration of the trade union movement as a public interest group, and the framework for negotiation provided by the Trade Disputes Act of 1966. This legislation requires both parties to an industrial dispute to enter into peaceful negotiation within a period of three weeks, and makes any agreement legally binding. In case of failure to reach agreement, either party has the right to request that the Commissioner of Labour mediate the dispute. If mediation fails, the dispute can be referred to arbitration by the Commissioner of Labour provided both parties agree to this. In cases where a work stoppage is likely to have serious negative social and economic effects, consent of the parties affected is not mandatory for arbitration.

Most of the legislation described above provides protection to workers already organised into trade unions. However, the majority of workers in the Sudan are not members of a trade union. Consequently, some attention has been given to protective labour legislation that would consider basic needs of these workers. Pre-independence statutes covered such areas as apprenticeship, workmen's compensation, domestic servants, and wages. New legislation has replaced the older laws based on British colonial prototypes. These new statutes provide greater protection than their predecessors. A new Apprenticeship and Vocational Training Act came into effect in 1974, and in the same year a Minimum Standard of Wages Order displaced the old Wages Tribunals Ordinance of 1952.

3 An Economic Overview

A CURRENT ECONOMIC SETTING

According to United Nations terminology, the Sudan is one of the twenty-five least developed countries. These countries embrace a total population of 150 million persons, and a land area of 11 million square miles.[1] The Sudan shares the following economic and related characteristics with these countries: (*a*) per capita Gross Domestic Product (GDP) of approximately $100, (*b*) a share of manufacturing in GDP of 10 per cent or less, (*c*) illiteracy of 75 per cent or higher, and (*d*) a low *per capita* level of electric power consumption. Africa accounts for 16 of these 25 countries, and the Sudan is among the largest of all countries designated as least developed (Table 3-1). The economic development prospects of these countries are hampered by poor physical infrastructure, lack of trained manpower, and a shortage of resources for investment.

The Sudan compares favourably with most other countries in the least developed category in terms of *per capita* GDP ($130). Moreover, during the decade of the 1960s growth in GDP and exports was satisfactory.[2] Sudan's economy is heavily dependent on agricultural production (40 per cent of GDP in 1971), and exports of agricultural and primary products account for a substantial part of GDP (25.4 per cent in 1971). The Sudan suffers from a lack of well-developed internal transportation facilities. However, road improvements and extension projects have been included in the most recently implemented economic development plan.

As of 1972 approximately one-fourth of the population of the Sudan lived in the modern sector, and three-fourths in the traditional sector. The distinction between the modern and traditional sectors hinges on methods and conditions of production, scale of economic activity, and extent to which monetary incentives influence economic activities. Close on 85 per cent of the population derives its livelihood from primary industry activity, including herding and cultivation of crops.[3] A large part of the population engaged

TABLE 3-1 Economic and Social Characteristics of Sixteen Least Developed Countries in Africa[a]

Country	Population (m.)	GNP ($US m.)	Per capita GNP $US	Growth rate 1960–73: Popul. %	Growth rate 1960–73: GNP per capita %	Share of manufact. in GDP[b] %	Avg. annual growth rate of food prod.	Adult literacy in 1968[d] %	US$ aid receipts (av. 1969–71): per capita	US$ aid receipts (av. 1969–71): As % of GNP
Sudan	17.0	2260	130	2.8	−0.9	11	−1.0	12	0.69	0.62
Botswana	0.6	150	230	1.9	4.7	11	—	20	24.21	—
Burundi	3.5	270	80	2.0	1.3	5	1.2	10	5.02	9.99
Chad	3.8	320	80	1.8	−2.1	8	−6.6	7	6.68	11.13
Dahomey	2.9	330	110	2.7	1.0	7	0.0	10	6.79	8.49
Ethiopia	26.5	2290	90	2.2	2.4	11	0.0	5	1.95	2.80
Guinea	5.2	570	110	2.8	0.1	6	−0.3	5	6.41	7.12
Lesotho	1.1	120	100	2.2	3.8	1	−11.2	40	13.76	17.20
Malawi	4.8	530	110	2.6	3.5	14	5.1	15	7.24	14.48
Mali	5.4	370	70	2.1	1.0	12	−0.9	2	4.86	5.40
Niger	4.3	450	100	2.7	−1.9	6	0.5	1	9.31	13.30
Rwanda	4.0	290	70	3.4	0.3	4	2.7	10	5.86	8.37
Somalia	3.0	250	80	2.4	−0.2	9	1.1	5	11.81	19.69
United Repub. Tanzania	13.9	1830	130	2.9	2.8	9	0.0	17	4.28	5.36
Uganda	10.8	1610	150	2.8	2.1	6	0.7	25	3.13	2.85
Upper Volta	5.7	410	70	2.1	−0.4	10	−0.9	7	4.31	—

[a] All data refer to year 1973, unless otherwise indicated.
[b] Refers to 1970.
[c] Refers to 1961–9.
[d] Data for Sudan covers period 1960–70.

SOURCE World Bank, *World Bank Atlas 1975*, p. 14; United Nations, *Industrial Development Survey*, 1974, p. 262; United Nations, *Survey of Conditions in Africa 1972*, Part I, 1973, p. 9.

in primary industry activities follows a traditional pattern, and relies on hand-operated irrigation methods or scarce rainfall. By contrast, the modern sector has adopted power-operated or gravity-flow methods of irrigation and the use of mechanical implements.

While most of the population engaged in agricultural pursuits produce primarily for their own subsistence, many market their surplus when the opportunity presents itself. Moreover, much of the agricultural output in the modern sector is used for subsistence.[4] Some cultivators and herders that produce largely for their own use regularly sell products such as gum arabic, sesame, or groundnuts in the commercial markets to supplement their livelihood. In the central region of the Sudan there is a considerable seasonal movement from traditional activities (nomadic herding and subsistence cultivation) to employment for wages on the large irrigated and mechanised agricultural developments.

Dualism is an important feature of the economic and social structure in the Sudan. Economic dualism refers to a situation where both traditional and modern economic sectors exist in the same country. In less developed countries the advanced exchange sector is characterised by well-functioning markets where money transactions predominate. At the same time a traditional sector operates wherein economic units are largely self-sufficient, where barter persists, and money plays at best a minor role.

Dualism can refer to social, technological, and financial as well as economic aspects. Technological dualism in the Sudan refers to the different technologies of production used in the modern and traditional sectors, e.g., deep-well irrigation pumps versus hand-operated pumps. Financial dualism refers to the distinctions that can be made between advanced financial institutions (commercial banks and central bank) and backward financial institutions (merciless moneylenders charging 150 per cent interest per annum). All aspects of dualism are evident in the Sudan.

In the Sudan the modern sector received its impetus with the introduction of cotton production in the irrigated areas in the 1920s. By the late 1960s the modern sector accounted for half of total output, and provided one-third of overall employment.[5] While much of the literature on dualism in less developed countries points to the modern sector as producing for export and the traditional sector producing for subsistence, this distinction is not strictly applicable to the Sudan. Most crops grown by the Gezira tenants (except cotton) are for subsistence. Nevertheless, the Gezira has been a core of the modern sector. Moreover, a major export product, gum arabic, is produced within the traditional sector.

The government has played an increasingly important role in the expansion of economic activity, and in the development of new areas of employment and income-yielding opportunities. Due to the scarcity of private savings the government has assumed a primary role in investing in infrastructure, agriculture, and industry. When the Sudan achieved independence in 1956 the government took over operation of the cotton marketing boards. A fall-off in the level of government investment after completion of major irrigation projects in the early 1960s resulted in a slower pace of economic growth over the period 1965–70. With the implementation of nationalization policy in 1970, the government has taken over all commercial banks, and medium and large-sized manufacturing firms that constitute the core of the modern industrial sector.

As in most developing countries, the Sudan chronically suffers from disguised underemployment (too many workers producing barely enough to live on). However, underemployment is not considered to be a severe problem in the Sudan as it is in many other developing countries. In fact the Sudan suffers from seasonal shortages of labour in the modern sector of agriculture, resulting in escalated wages and migration of workers from other parts of Africa. There continue to be sectoral shortages of skilled urban labour, and in the past a high proportion of skilled jobs and managerial positions has been filled by foreigners.

An analysis of higher education in 21 selected least developed countries indicates that the Sudan ranked second among these countries in number of students in higher education per 100,000 population (70 per 100,000 population in 1966).[6] The largest enrolments of Sudanese students in higher education included the non-technical disciplines, engineering, teaching, natural sciences, and medicine, in that order. Business administration apparently was not emphasised in higher education in these countries.

The potential for economic advancement in the Sudan appears favourable, given the required political and social stability. The country's international credit-worthiness has been enhanced with (*a*) the termination of war with the southern rebels in 1972, (*b*) modest achievements toward diversification of industrial structure initiated in the 1960s, and (*c*) the improved yield and stability of cotton productivity. In the five year period 1967–72 the Sudan consistently maintained a high level of cotton production, offering evidence that organised activity and investment in cotton growing could yield a stable pattern of returns for the national economy and the cultivator.

B NATIONAL INCOME AND ECONOMIC GROWTH

1 *Growth in Output*

Government development policies must be shaped in light of evidence concerning past economic growth, current problems, and prospects for the future. Therefore, it is important that reasonably reliable statistical estimates be available concerning past and present success and failure. Development policies that are suitable for a growing economy may be totally ill-suited for one that is in a state of menopause.

Difficulties abound when one attempts to analyse the relative success achieved in the economic growth of the Sudan. These are occasioned by faulty statistics, data gaps, and a lack of comprehensive data gathering by the government and semi-official agencies. We have already commented on this problem in the discussion of population and manpower data in Chapter 2. This difficulty becomes magnified when attempting to measure the growth of output in the Sudan. At best we can hope to obtain an impressionistic 'feel' for the situation.

Data published on an official basis carries sobering conclusions regarding Sudan's economic advance since independence. Data contained in Table 3-2 suggests that in the period 1960–73 total output

TABLE 3-2 Growth in Population and Output *per capita* (Annual Rates)

	1960–73	*1965–73*
Population	2.8	2.8
GNP *per capita*	−0.9	−0.6
Total output	1.9	2.2

SOURCE *World Bank Atlas*, 1975, pp. 14–15.

has increased by only 1.9 per cent per annum, and that on a *per capita* basis there has been some retrogression. These figures appear surprising considering the impressive advances made by the Sudan in irrigated and mechanised agriculture (described in Chapter 4). For this reason, it is worth comparing the results in Table 3-2 with the data available on agricultural production and cultivated acreage. Data on crop production and acreage offer the advantages of not requiring deflation for price level changes, and do not lend themselves to *per capita* adjustments which can be misleading where population data is subject to a wide range of estimates.

Data available on the growth of agricultural output (Table 3-3) in the Sudan suggest that in the two-decade period ending in 1975 acreage and production increased nearly fourfold. This data includes the major agricultural crops in terms of value of output, contribution to export earnings, and employment and income opportunities. Available statistics on the number of animals slaughtered tell a similar story. In the same two-decade period cattle slaughterings

TABLE 3-3 Growth of Agricultural Production in Sudan, 1951/52–1955/56 to 1974/75

	% Increase in production	*Production in 1974/75 (000 tons)*	*Area under Cultivation 1974/75 (000 feddans)*
Cotton	166	670	1,168
Dura (Sorghum)	186	1,875	5,764
Groundnuts	2,731	991	1,987
Sesame	198	271	1,976
Wheat	1,805	362	620
Total		4,169	11,515
Average for 1951/52–1955/56		1,052	3,049

SOURCE *Economic Survey 1957* and *Economic Survey 1974*, Democratic Republic of the Sudan.

have increased fivefold.[7] The preceding indicates that growth in agricultural production has been a sustained feature of the Sudan's development and that data contained in official national income accounts must be used with care and discretion.

2 *Macro Data*

Official estimates of the Sudan's gross domestic product for the period 1960–70 are reproduced in Table 3-4. The major expenditure categories have shifted in relative importance over the years, with an increase in the share of government expenditure almost matched by a decline in the share of private consumption expenditures. Changes in inventories (increase in stocks) display an expected volatility. Gross capital formation also displays a tendency to fluctuate. Public investment accounts for slightly over half of total investment, and its share of the total has fluctuated as a result of the inherent lumpiness of major public works projects and due to the need at times for government economy measures to achieve better economic and financial equilibrium. Exports are nearly as volatile as capital formation, reflecting both price and volume changes of important export commodities (cotton, groundnuts and gum arabic) in world markets. Imports have exceeded exports in nine of the eleven years reflected in Table 3-4. Import volumes change markedly on a year-to-year basis due to application of more stringent or more relaxed licensing and quota policies by the national government.

TABLE 3-4 Gross Domestic Product in the Sudan, percentage composition 1960–70

Year	*Gross Domestic Product £S. m.*	*Govt. expenditure*	*Private consump. expendit.*	*Increase in stocks*	*Gross Fixed capital formation*	*Exports of goods and services*	*Imports of goods and services*
		Percentage of GDP					
1960	386.8	8	79	1	11	17	16
1961	420.0	9	78	3	13	15	18
1962	456.2	9	76	2	14	17	19
1963	464.1	10	78	−1	16	19	23
1964	476.8	12	78	0	14	18	22
1965	496.9	13	77	2	11	17	19
1966	497.6	19	69	1	14	18	21
1967	536.3	20	69	0	13	17	20
1968	583.2	19	70	2	12	18	21
1969	602.6	25	58	0	16	19	17
1970	637.6	25	63	3	11	19	21

SOURCE United Nations, *Yearbook of National Accounts Statistics*, 1974, Volume III.

3. *Gross Capital Formation*

Gross domestic capital formation has fluctuated between 11 per cent and 16 per cent of GDP (Table 3-4). There does not appear to be any clear trend for this component to increase or decline as a per cent of GDP. In the period 1966–70 gross capital formation increased from £S.75.6 million to £S.89.6 million (Table 3-5). Over the period 1966–70 domestic saving has provided 42 per cent of the financing of gross capital formation, capital consumption 45 per cent, and capital transfers from the rest of the world the remaining 12 per cent of the total.

During the five-year period 1966–70 gross fixed capital formation averaged £S.76 million annually, approximately 13 per cent of GDP. The major components by type of capital goods were: machinery and equipment, which averaged £S.23 million per annum or 30 per cent of fixed capital formation; transport equipment, which averaged £S.16 million per annum or 21 per cent of fixed capital formation; residential and non-residential construction, which averaged £S.19 million or 25 per cent of fixed capital formation; land improvements and orchard development which averaged £S.2 million per annum or 3 per cent of capital formation; and other construction excluding land improvements, which averaged £S.10 million per annum or 13 per cent of capital formation (Table 3-5).

TABLE 3-5 Composition of Gross Capital Formation 1966–70 (£S.m.)

	1966	*1967*	*1968*	*1969*	*1970*
1. Residential buildings				15.7	16.3
2. Non-residential buildings	17.4	15.9	18.0	16.7	
				10.9	2.4
3. Other construction	8.6	9.0	10.9	12.8	
				13.4	8.1
4. Land improvement, plantation,	3.4	1.8	0.9	19.5	
and orchard development				3.7	1.8
5. Transport equipment	11.1	12.7	13.5	5.9	
				20.6	23.7
6. Machinery and equipment	23.8	20.5	23.8	15.3	
				31.3	20.9
7. Breeding stocks and cattle	3.2	3.3	3.7	0.2	
				0.3	—
8. Statistical discrepancy	4.4	7.3	—	—	—
9. Gross fixed capital formation	71.8	70.4	70.9	70.5	
				96.0	73.2
10. Goods producing industries, stock	4.1	5.4	4.2	7.5	
accumulation				8.6	11.3
10a. Materials and supplies	1.7	0.8	1.3	1.5	
				5.5	7.9
10b. Work in progress				0.2	
				0.7	0.5
10c. Livestock and cattle	1.7	2.3	2.2	4.7	
				—	—
10d. Finished goods	0.8	2.3	0.7	1.0	
				2.4	2.9
11. Wholesale and retail trade,	2.5	2.2	5.0	6.0	
stock accumulation				−8.9	3.4
12. Other industries, stock	−2.9	−5.0	0.8	1.2	
accumulation				—	1.8
13. Government stock accumulation	3.8	2.6	0.9	14.6	
				−0.3	16.4
14. Gross capital formation	75.6	73.1	80.8	85.1	
				95.7	89.6

SOURCE United Nations, *Yearbook of National Accounts Statistics*, 1974, Volume III. For 1969 values 15.7 and 10.9 belong to the second series.

4 *Gross Domestic Product by Industrial Origin*

The industrial origin of GDP has been exposed to significant structural change since 1960. The contribution of agriculture has declined from 57 per cent in 1960 to 40 per cent in 1971. By contrast the shares of industry and services increased, with services displaying the most pronounced gain in share of GDP (from 27 per cent in 1960 to 42 per cent in 1971). Within the industry sector manufacturing increased its contribution to GDP from 5 per cent in 1960 to 9 per cent in 1971.

The cost structure of GDP also has undergone significant structural changes. By 1970 consumption of fixed capital increased to two-and-one-half times its level a decade earlier, reflecting the substantial accumulation of capital over the decade. A second important change in the cast structure of GDP was the doubling of indirect taxes. In part this resulted from an increase in tax revenues on international trade, reflecting rapid expansion in the foreign trade sector.

C CONSUMER SPENDING AND THE PROPENSITY TO CONSUME

As noted in an earlier section of this chapter the Sudan is characterised by dualism in most aspects of economic and social activity. Economic dualism has important implications for government policy, the pattern of consumption expenditure, and real investment opportunities. In the discussion which follows we examine the propensity to consume in the Sudan, consider sectoral-regional differences in the propensity to consume, and the significance of dualism for the country's economic development.

Over the period 1955–67 the share of consumer spending in disposable income was quite stable, remaining within a range of 89.8 to 98.4 per cent of disposable income (Table 3-6). In this period the year-to-year variation in average propensity to consume never exceeded 5.7 per cent (in 1966–7). The data for the entire period reflect an average propensity to consume for the Sudanese economy of 93 per cent. This is somewhat higher than the APC found in Egypt and Ceylon, where the subsistence sector is smaller; and somewhat lower than the APC in Nigeria, where the traditional sector is very large.[8] Fitting a regression line to the disposable income and consumer expenditures data yields a marginal propensity to consume of 0.89.[9]

The APC and MPC values derived for the Sudan provide valuable information concerning saving and economic growth prospects. Moreover, the level of consumption is relevant to the adoption of appropriate stabilisation policies. High levels of consumption make efforts at avoiding economic recession much easier. Alternately, in periods of inflation high levels of consumer spending make it more difficult to repress spending by means of market-oriented economic policies. The level of consumption also is important in connection with investment decisions. This is especially the case where the level of sales influences investment decisions. Finally, the MPC plays a vital role in the multiplier process. Given a high MPC, incremental investment will exert greater leverage on income.

In less developed countries such as the Sudan both the marginal and average propensities to consume tend to be high, in part

TABLE 3-6 Relationship between Consumer Spending and Income in the Sudan, 1955–67

Year	*Average propensity to consume (APC)*	*Share of private consumption in GDP (%)*
1955	89.8	96
1956	90.3	86
1957	92.5	91
1958	90.9	81
1959	93.9	87
1960	93.7	77
1961	91.0	71
1962	91.9	70
1963	93.1	76
1964	91.0	65
1965	96.1	69
1966	92.7	79
1967	98.4	71

SOURCE Mohamed Abdel Rahman Ali, 'The Propensity to Consume and Economic Development in a Dual Economy: Sudan 1955–67', *Sudan Notes and Records* (Khartoum, 1972), pp. 118 and 124.

because the relatively large traditional sector influences these propensities, and because internal and external demonstration effects tend to be substantial.[10]

The high marginal propensity to consume observed in the Sudan does not necessarily generate strong income expansion (cumulative process) effects. This is accounted for by the dual nature of the Sudanese economy, and money income leakages. Economic dualism is characterised in the Sudan by a traditional sector that accounts for nearly half of total output. Within this traditional sector are 'large self-contained groups which are outside the monetary economy altogether' and which remain largely unaffected by changes in expenditures levels in the modern sector. In this case the traditional sector in the Sudan will absorb money income generated by a multiplier expansion but not immediately respend this income in successive rounds of expenditures. In short, the respending chain becomes broken. One writer offers several reasons for expecting a less powerful multiplier in dual economies.[11] These include the disincentives to traditional sector investment resulting from export sector investment, and the lower productivity in the traditional as compared with the modern sector.

Money income leakages play an important role in the Sudan due to the large number of transients that take up temporary residence. This group of migrant workers consists in large part of West African muslims who spend many years undertaking the religious pilgrimage to Mecca. These individuals take up residence in countries such as Chad and the Sudan while on the pilgrimage. During their residence in the Sudan they may be occupied as labourers, farm helpers, or street merchants. A considerable portion of their cash earnings is hoarded to cover expenses that will be incurred during the next leg of their journey.[12] As a result, a significant leakage of cash income takes place.

Table 3-6 also depicts private consumption as a share of GDP. During the period 1955–67 the percentage share of consumption displayed marked fluctuations. Over the entire period the share of consumption in GDP declined. Nevertheless, private consumption increased in absolute real terms in almost every year. The declining share of private consumption was matched by an increase in public consumption expenditure.

Aggregate consumption propensities conceal important sectoral and regional differences. The propensity to consume in the traditional sector is very high and may in some cases exceed unity. In the modern sector, where incomes are relatively high the propensity to consume is lower. Moreover, there are substantial differences in the average propensity to consume in the cities and in the rural parts of the modern sector such as the Gezira.[13] In the Gezira the APC is lower than the average for the Sudan. Therefore it has been found that saving is much higher in the Gezira than in other regions of the Sudan.

Sectoral and regional differences in the propensity to consume have importat implications for economic development. The high average propensity to consume offers a potential market for private investment undertakings. This is important since it is widely assumed that low savings rather than low profits hinder private investment. If this is true, government policies should be less concerned with a concentration of relatively high incomes in the modern sector since this could become a major contributor to the flow of saving and investment.

D SAVING AND INVESTMENT

The major economic problem of the Sudan has been and still is its excessive dependence on cultivation and export of a few agricultural products. Broadening of the Sudanese economic structure through the development of service and manufacturing industries has been an important aspect of the overall economic development strategy of the Sudanese government.

Saving and investment have presented opportunities as well as obstacles to the economic development process in the Sudan. Lack of adequate saving has imposed a dependence on external sources of investment funds, and further required that government fiscal policy be geared toward financing a major share of the accumulation of capital. Through the period 1960–70 fixed capital formation has represented a modest 11–13 per cent of GDP (Table 3-7). Even if we allow for the increase in stocks (inventory accumulation), the ratios in Table 3-7 for the period 1966–70 do not rise significantly

TABLE 3-7 Fixed Capital Formation in the Sudan as a percentage of Gross Domestic Product, 1956–70

1956–59	9.4
1960–5	13.3
1966–9	12.9
1970	11.4

SOURCE United Nations, *Yearbook of National Accounts Statistics*, relevant years.

above 13 per cent. There are several reasons for the low ratio of capital formation relative to GDP. These include the low level of *per capita* income which dampens opportunities for savings, the absence of a large competitive business enterprise sector to initiate more profitable investments, the inability of the government to initiate a larger number of investment projects, the scarcity of infrastructure, and limits on the ability of the economy to attract foreign source capital in larger amount.

The capital-output ratio affords an overview of the contribution of savings-investment to the growth rate. Estimates of the incremental capital-output ratio (ICOR) are difficult. Using the familiar expression

$$g = \frac{s}{k} - p$$

to reflect the potential growth in real *per capita* income, where s represents the saving ratio (saving as a percentage of GDP), k the incremental capital-output ratio, and p the growth trend in population, we can estimate the potential growth for the Sudan. Inserting values of 13 per cent for s, 2.6 for k,[14] and 2.8 per cent for p, we obtain a potential annual growth of *per capita* income equal to 2.2 per cent.

The initiative for undertaking capital investments in the Sudan has been shared almost equally between the private and public sectors. This applies to experience recorded for the latter half of the 1960s, as well as in blueprints embodied in the five-year develop-

TABLE 3-8A Capital Investments of the Public Sector (US$m.)

	1965/66–1969/70	*1970/71–1974/75*	*Average annual increase (%)*	*% share* *1965/66–1969/70*	*% share* *1970/71–1974/75*
Agriculture	137.6	220.1	9.9	34.8	38.3
Industry	25.3	75.8	24.6	6.4	13.2
Power	35.9	36.8	0.6	9.0	6.4
Transport and communications	69.5	85.1	4.1	17.6	14.8
Education and culture	24.1	41.9	11.7	6.1	7.3
Health	13.2	24.1	12.7	3.4	4.2
Public utilities	24.1	37.4	9.3	6.1	6.6
Halfa resettlement	12.9	—	—	3.3	—
Central administration	15.5	18.5	3.4	4.0	3.2
Unallocated	—	6.6	—	—	1.1
Technical assistance and grants	37.3	28.1	−5.9	9.3	4.9
Total	395.4	571.4*	7.7	100.0	100.0

* Excluding a $43.1 m. loan.

TABLE 3–8B Capital Investments of the Private Sector (US$ m.)

Agriculture	36.8	76.1	15.6	10.2	15.6
Industry	50.8	68.9	6.3	14.0	14.1
Housing	203.3	226.3	2.1	56.3	46.4
Road transport	64.0	89.0	6.8	17.7	18.2
Education	2.0	20.7	−44.0	0.6	4.2
Health		5.2	10.8	1.2	1.1
Miscellaneous	4.3	2.0	—	—	0.4
Total	361.2	488.2	6.2	100.0	100.0

SOURCE UNIDO, *Summaries of Industrial Development Plans*, Vol. III (1973), pp. 342–3.

ment plan for 1970–5. In the five-year period 1965–70 the private sector financed 48 per cent of capital investments, and in the five-year development plan for 1970–5 the private sector was scheduled to finance 46 per cent of capital investments.[15] Approximately half of public sector capital investment was scheduled to be financed by foreign sources of funds during the period 1970–5.

In Table 3-8A and 3-8B we have detailed comparisons of capital investments undertaken by the public and private sectors for the five-year periods 1965–70 (actual) and 1970–5 (economic development plan). Examining the data on public sector capital investments we should note that the economic development plan for 1970–5 provided for a 7.7 per cent annual increase in investment. The most important categories of investment were agriculture, transport and communications, and industry, accounting for 38.3 per cent, 14.8 per cent, and 13.2 per cent of planned investment respectively. The largest percentage increase in investment was designated for the industry category (24.6 per cent annual increase). Other important categories in terms of share of funds appropriated for capital investment included education, public utilities, and power.

Investments in the private sector were scheduled to increase by a somewhat narrower margin of 6.2 per cent annually over the five-year period 1970–5. In the private sector investment in housing represented the largest single category of capital accumulation in both five-year periods. This is essentially household sector investment. Three other important investment categories in the private sector included road transport, agriculture, and industry, constituting 18.2, 15.6, and 14.1 per cent respectively.

4 Agriculture and Forestry

A GENERAL IMPORTANCE

At present the two key economic sectors in the Sudan are transport and agriculture. Agricultural production is the major marketable commodity of the Sudan and transportation is required to get this product to the market places of the world. In addition to its strategic importance as a net earner of foreign exchange, agriculture exerts a tremendous quantitative impact on the fortunes (or vicissitudes) of the Sudan. Agriculture contributes close to 40 per cent of Gross Domestic Product, generates over 90 per cent of the Sudan's merchandise exports, provides the bulk of raw materials needed for local industries, and provides employment opportunities for over three-fourths of the work force.[1]

Approximately 200 million feddans of the total area of the Sudan (625 million feddans) is considered suitable for crop or pastoral farming. At the present time one-half of this area is being used for growing crops and for pastoral activities, largely in an unsystematic fashion. As of 1975 approximately 16 million feddans were under cultivation, and of this about 4 million acres were irrigated.[2]

A great variety of agricultural crops can be grown in the Sudan, including cotton, grains, fruits and vegetables. A basic constraint on agricultural production is availability of water. For this reason expansion of agricultural production has taken place along the Nile, its main tributaries, and in the regions of the Sudan endowed with adequate rainfall.

There are three main types of agriculture practised in the Sudan. These include irrigated agriculture, rain-fed agriculture, and traditional agriculture. Irrigated agriculture is limited mainly to the area lying between the Blue and White Nile, and smaller areas along the Atbara and Rahad Rivers. In these areas long-staple cotton, groundnuts, wheat, and fruits and vegetables are cultivated. Rain-fed agriculture is carried out mainly in the region east of the Blue Nile in the general area of Gedaref, and in southern Kordofan

Province. A large part of this activity is mechanised and very extensive land areas are involved. Production is concentrated in sorghum, sesame, and short-staple cotton. In recent years wheat, groundnuts, and sesame production has increased rapidly in these rain-fed regions. Traditional agriculture is carried out in the central and western areas of the Sudan, as well as in all of the southern region. Very little surplus product is available for market. Livestock production has remained organised along traditional lines and consequently limits the return accruing to the livestock producer.

Mechanisation of Sudanese agriculture is reflected in Table 4-1 (lines 1 and 2). It is expected that additional mechanisation will become necessary due to some tightening up in the labour market, lower mobility of workers, and increased need for the achievement of high productivity. Rationalisation is taking place in Sudanese agriculture as marginal land is shifted from cotton cultivation to uses where greater overall productivity can be attained or where self-sufficiency can be promoted. The flat series (Table 4-1) for cotton production reflects shifting use of land away from cotton in established cultivated areas and increased acreage use in more recently developed agricultural regions. Some of the land taken out of cotton cultivation has been shifted to wheat or sugar production. During the 1960s the Gezira witnessed a considerable expansion in wheat acreage.[3]

Sudan gums have been known in world trade for at least two thousand years. Gum arabic, which constituted between 5 and 10 per cent of Sudan's exports in the period 1969–73, has long been a leading source of export revenue. While collected in the traditional sector it is purely a cash crop. Virtually all of the gum arabic produced in the Sudan is exported. Sudan is the world's largest source of gum arabic, with 75 to 85 per cent of total world output.[4] Kordofan and Darfur Provinces in western Sudan are the main production centres of gum arabic. In 1969 the government formed the Gum Arabic Exporting Company Ltd, a public company in which the government participation was at 30 per cent of the capital. This company now handles all of the gum trade of the Sudan with the objectives of improving the distribution, stabilising prices, and maximising the returns earned by the Sudan on gum exports.

Agricultural production enters into the foreign trade of the Sudan in an important way. Virtually all of the Sudan's merchandise exports is made up of agricultural products. Exports of cotton constitute 55–60 per cent of exports, oil seed and oil cake exports constitute another 17 per cent and 6 per cent of exports, respectively. Exports of gum arabic have accounted for 8–10 per cent of exports. Finally, livestock products make up another 7 per cent of merchandise exports. On the import side agricultural products also

TABLE 4-1 Selected Statistics on the Growth of Agriculture in the Sudan

	1952–56	*1961*	*1965*	*1967*	*1969*	*1970*	*1973*	*1974*
1. No. Tractors in use	215	2,040*	2,300	3,000	4,462	4,848	8,000	n.a.
2. No. Combined harvester-thresher in use	8	120*	140	150	230	300	700	n.a
3. Cotton Lint production	87	148	152	188	228	246	190	229
4. Wheat production	19	26	56	78	123	115	152	235
5. Cattle production	5,619	8,052*	10,012	12,115	13,326	13,800	15,200	14,000
6. Sheep production	6,237	8,255*	9,526	11,562	12,678	13,500	15,400	11,900
7. Groundnut production	61	329*	305	322	383	337	636	991

* Covers period 1961–65.

Data on lines 1 and 2 are in number of units. Data in line 3 are in metric tons. Data on lines 4 and 7 are thousand metric tons. Data on lines 5 and 6 are in thousands of head.

SOURCE: United Nations, *Statistical Yearbook*; FAO, *Production Yearbook*.

play a significant role, representing one-fourth of total merchandise imports. This has imposed a strain on the balance of payments and necessitated imposition of self-sufficiency objectives in the production of currently imported agricultural commodities (sugar and wheat).

In the Sudan modern agriculture has been carried out largely under the authority of state corporations. In the irrigated areas this has meant that management and innovation has been effected through such agencies as the Gezira Board and Rahad Corporation. In the regions where dry farming (rain-fed) has dominated, the Mechanised Farming Corporation has functioned as a central organisational unit. In addition several state enterprises have provided specialised services to producers. For example, the Cotton Public Corporation and Gum Arabic Corporation have provided monopolistic purchasing, marketing, and distributing power over crops produced. In addition, the Ministry of Agriculture has developed into a well-staffed unit providing a wide range of important and useful services. Similarly, the Ministry of Irrigation and Hydroelectric Power has taken the initiative in water management and operation of large-scale irrigation schemes.

B. IRRIGATED AGRICULTURE

1 *Organisation and Extent of Irrigated Areas*

Modern irrigated agriculture is relatively new in the Sudan, dating from 1925 when the Sennar Dam was completed. The damming of the Blue Nile permitted gravity irrigation of extensive areas of cotton planting. The Gezira Irrigation Scheme originally was managed by private businessmen, but was nationalised after World War II and placed under the control of the then newly formed Sudan Gezira Board.

Various types of irrigation schemes operate in the Sudan. These include the large schemes, each covering several hundred thousand acres, and managed by government bodies. In these schemes cultivation is carried out largely by tenants. The Gezira and Rahad are probably the best known of this type irrigation scheme. In addition there are smaller pump schemes, some initiated by private operators, some nationalised by the Agrarian Reform Corporation. A number of pump schemes on the Nile River north of Khartoum are managed by the Northern Province Agricultural Corporation. Finally, there is a large number of small irrigation schemes spread across various parts of the Sudan. Some of these are fed by deep bore wells and others by pumped river water.

As of 1972 approximately 2.2 million feddans of land area were under irrigation in the Gezira–Managil, an additional 1.4 million feddans in pump schemes south of Khartoum, some 400,000 feddans by gravity irrigation in the Kashm el Girba, and about 70,000 feddans along the Nile north of Khartoum. As of 1973 close to 40 per cent of the irrigated land in the Gezira–Managil area was allocated to cotton growing, with another 20 per cent devoted to sorghum. Wheat and groundnuts, with approximately equal land area in cultivation, together absorbed another 20 per cent of irrigated land area. The remaining cultivated land area under irrigation is used for growing of vegetables, onions, sugarcane, citrus and other crops.

2. *Gezira-Managil Scheme*

The Gezira is a large, flat plain lying south of Khartoum between the Blue and White Niles. The idea of developing the Gezira by gravity irrigation followed publication of a report on the Upper Nile Basin in 1904. This report advocated a barrage dam at Sennar on the Blue Nile.[5] In the 1910–11 growing season commercial cotton was grown on approximately 250 feddans at Tayiba. In the following two seasons cotton acreage was increased, and in 1913 funds were raised with British Treasury guarantee to construct the Sennar Dam. Construction was delayed due to the outbreak of World War I. Construction was resumed in 1919 and the dam was completed and officially opened in 1925.

Arthur Gaitskell, first chairman and managing director of the Sudan Gezira Board, has noted that the Gezira Scheme was planned in the spirit of trusteeship, based on the belief that stability and permanence of economic investment depends on the 'contentment of the people'. He noted further,[6]

> In underdeveloped countries the need for an ordered plan to overcome poverty is extremely difficult to avoid. The problem is to get off the ground floor of mere subsistence, but also to see that the benefit does not remain merely in a few hands, leaving a great rift between enterprising rich and feckless poor.

The Gezira is organised as a tripartite partnership with the Sudan Gezira Board (SGB), the tenants, and government sharing in management and policy making. The SGB and government share major responsibility for establishing cropping patterns, rotation, and prices. Size of the 96,000 tenancies ranges between 40 feddans in the old section to 15 feddans in the newer Managil extension.

Costs and revenues are shared between the three parties according to a complicated formula. In general the tenant pays for direct cultivation costs including levelling, weeding, sowing and cleaning. Ploughing and initial watering are charged to a joint account, as is the cost of cotton picking. The costs of supplying irrigation water and canal maintenance are borne by the Ministry of Irrigation. The

SGB meets the cash expenses of ploughing, seeds, fertilisers, collection of seed cotton and its transportation, ginning and transport; but includes these in the joint account.

While the joint account system has appeared to work well, several problems exist. First, there is no strong incentive for tenants to improve crop yields. Second, supply of farm labour has posed problems. Tenants prefer to hire labour rather than make use of members of the family (tenant families have an average size of seven members, but contribute on average only 1.5 workers per tenancy). Consequently, migrant workers travel long distances to work in the Gezira on a seasonal basis. This represents an uneconomic use and management of Sudan's labour force. Third, it is becoming more difficult to attract migrant labour. As economic development takes place and modern agriculture grows in those regions of the Sudan now supplying migrant workers on a seasonal basis, more attractive job opportunities will emerge and it will become increasingly difficult to attract low-cost migrant workers.

The Sudan Gezira Board is in the process of reallocating land under cultivation. This involves a reduction in cotton acreage of about one-third, and increases in land area devoted to growing wheat and groundnuts. This change would alleviate the seasonal demand for farm labour, provide a greater self-sufficiency in food products, possibly improve the merchandise trade balance on agricultural goods, reduce the dependence of the Sudan on cotton exports and the vagaries of world demand, and improve on the ability of SGB to mechanise harvesting (grains and groundnuts). Land utilisation would become more diversified, and more intensified methods of cultivation would become possible.

The move toward diversification, intensification and mechanisation of agriculture in the Gezira–Managil Scheme poses several additional problems. It will be necessary to increase the use of fertilisers to maintain soil fertility as well as increase yields per feddan. This represents an increased foreign exchange outlay.[7] Also, a mechanisation project has been developed that would require importation of tractors and harvesters.[8] Finally and perhaps most significant, water requirements will expand. There are several facets to the increased water requirements. First, main conduit canals may not have adequate water delivery capacity in the peak requirement period. Possible solutions to this problem include revised cropping patterns and expanding the capacity of several canals. Second, total water use will increase.

Over the past four decades the Gezira–Managil Scheme has increased its total consumption of Nile River waters by over 300 per cent. In 1939–40 total consumption was 1.56 billion cubic metres. With opening of the Managil Extension consumption rose to 3.7

billion cubic metres in 1964–5. It has been estimated that in 1974–5 consumption reached 6.85 billion cubic metres.[9] In 1974–5 total land area under irrigation in the Sudan was 4 million feddans, and Nile water consumption was 14.24 billion cubic metres. Under the 1959 Nile Waters Agreement the Sudan's allocation of 18.5 billion cubic metres at Aswan translates into 20.5 billion cubic metres of water at Khartoum. Projects under implementation and to be completed in the period 1975–80[10] will add approximately 1.64 billion cubic metres of water consumption, still leaving 4.62 billion cubic metres of slack. Agricultural intensification in the Gezira–Managil might add another 2.15 billion cubic metres of water consumption, reducing the surplus available under the Nile Waters Agreement to 2.47 billion cubic metres. Expansion plans for the early 1980s would more than use up this surplus, requiring that the Sudan invest considerable resources in providing additional Nile water. One source would be construction of the Jonglei Canal, which would extend from Jonglei where the White Nile enters the Sudan almost to Malakal (approximately 300 kilometres). The canal would reduce the flow of water through the Sud (a swampy area in the southern Sudan), and deliver more water through the Nile. An additional source of water would come from draining the Bhar El Ghazal. These additional sources of water would not quite make up the projected deficit in water needed for irrigation purposes into the mid-1980s.

3 *Rahad Scheme*

The Rahad Scheme involves developing a 300,000-fedden area of irrigated land on the east bank of the Rahad River. Water would be supplied by pump from the Blue Nile. It has been estimated that the Rahad Project will cost over $240 million and that six years will be required for construction to be completed. Approximately two-thirds of the cost represents foreign exchange requirements, most of which is to be provided by loans on a concessional basis.[11] Half of the area available for cultivation will be planted in cotton, and a third of the area in groundnuts.

The construction phase of the project is elaborate, entailing irrigation and drainage works, an electrically powered pumping station, an 84-kilometre supply canal, headquarters offices and housing, electrical stations and transmission facilities, and a road network. Additional facilities will include seed and research farms, and storage and processing facilities for cotton and groundnuts.

The Rahad Corporation Act (1972) provides that tenants in the scheme be charged a flat 'land and water charge' so that the government can recover annual expenses, obtain an adequate return on investment, and provide for depreciation. Moreover, the project is designed to permit the farmer to earn a cash income equal to the average family income in the Sudan. It is expected that close to 14,000 families will benefit from the project as farm tenants. In addition the scheme should provide employment for 90,000 workers.[12] Other benefits from the Rahad Project include a substantial increase in net foreign exchange earnings and export tax revenues to the central government, improved technology in agriculture, and a better trained staff of Sudanese to be utilised in future development schemes.

4 *Investment in Irrigation and Alternatives*

As noted in the preceding discussion the Sudan appears to be committed to an expansion of agricultural production by use of irrigated land. Irrigated acreage would increase by approximately 15 per cent over the period 1975–80, and by another 20 per cent in the period 1980–5.[13] In future expanding irrigated acreage in the Sudan will require increasing the availability of water (water storage, canals, and pump facilities) as well as providing infrastructure related directly to cultivation (roads, agricultural equipment, new housing, and investment in a management organisation). One alternative is to invest in the development of alternative agricultural schemes (mechanised dry farming). Another alternative is to concentrate on more intensified methods of farming in areas already under cultivation.

Calculations made by the World Bank in planning the Rahad Project provide comparisons of investment costs per feddan and per farm worker in the Sudan.[14] The general conclusion from these comparisons is that investment in irrigated farming costs ten times as much as in mechanised farming and twenty-five times as much as investment in traditional farming. A similar pattern is found if we examine investment cost per farm worker. Investment costs per worker in irrigated agriculture are seven times as large as in mechanised agriculture, and forty times as large as in traditional agriculture. Irrigation investment is extremely capital-intensive, and has the lowest net foreign exchange benefit (high import content of operations and external debt servicing). It is true that investment in irrigated agriculture probably has larger positive employment effects than investment in mechanised and traditional agriculture. The past record of success in irrigated agriculture in the Sudan has placed this approach in a favourable light among government officials and economic planners. However, future investment decisions in the field of agriculture will have to be made considering the relative value of alternative means of expanding crop production. Moreover, trade-off relationships will have to be taken into consideration including income effects, employment effects, comparative advantage, and achievement of regional balance in economic and social progress.

C MECHANISED AGRICULTURE

1 *Current Status*

Mechanised farming developed on a large scale in the Sudan in the 1950s. An important growth stimulant was a government policy decision to allot land to private entrepreneurs who cleared and improved the land themselves. Mechanised farming techniques were extended to regions with soil bearing a heavy clay content. These areas could not be cultivated efficiently by hand power due to the heavy clay content. In 1968 the government established the Mechanised Farming Corporation (MFC), which assumed responsibility for mechanised projects from the Agriculture Ministry. The MFC allocates land to private farmers who clear and prepare the land, and provide machinery. Also, MFC operates state farms directly.

Mechanised farming is concentrated in two provinces (Kassala and Blue Nile), although two other provinces have significant areas cultivated in this manner (Kordofan and Upper Nile). In 1973 approximately 60 per cent of the land area devoted to mechanised farming was located in Kassala Province. In terms of production tonnage, the major crop is sorghum, with sesame second in importance (Table 4-2).

TABLE 4-2 Area Cultivated and Production on Mechanised Farms 1973–4

	Area ('000 *feddans*)	*Production* ('000 *tons*)
Sorghum	2422	835
Sesame	730	108
Cotton	34	5.2
Total	3186	948.2

SOURCE: Mechanised Farming Corporation.

The mechanised farm area is over 4 million feddans, of which approximately three-fourths is in cultivation (not fallow) each year. Mechanisation is partial, in that most of the harvesting is done by hand labour.

Investment required by a farmer in a mechanised farm of 1500 feddans can be considerable. With a land clearing cost of £S.10 per feddan, and assuming only two-thirds of the land area is cleared, investment in land clearing is £S.10,000. Purchase of machinery may run to another £S.7000, and operating costs during the first year to another £S.2000, bringing the total investment to £S.19,000. Return on investment can also be sizeable. The farmer may earn an income of £S.4000 representing a 21 per cent return on investment. Naturally, crop risks are ever-present.

2. *Evaluation*

The development of mechanised farming in the Sudan has brought with it favourable effects in the areas of employment, foreign trade, and investment incentives. Alternatively, it has generated costs in the way of soil misuse and disruption of established social patterns. Employment effects also have been significant. In 1975 some 8000 permanent jobs were provided on mechanised farms, and another 500,000 seasonal jobs were made available.

It has been estimated that mechanised farming has a favourable effect on the foreign trade balance.[15] Imported fuel plus agricultural machinery (amortised) have a value of approximately one-third of the value of sorghum, sesame, and cotton grown on mechanised farms and available for export.

Mechanised farming attracts private investment in agriculture, and permits use of land resources that otherwise might not be cultivated. This is because the heavy clay soil could not be brought into cultivation without mechanised methods.

On the negative side mechanised farming does make soil depletion possible and there is strong argument for MFC undertaking soil analysis to detect poor farming practices. A solution to this problem would include planting of leguminous fodder crops. Another problem area focuses on the interference with seasonal movements of nomadic herds. It has been found possible to solve this problem by arranging for wide 'channels' through which herds can be driven to seasonal water points.

D LIVESTOCK

The Sudan possesses animal wealth which contributes about 10 per cent to GDP annually. It has been estimated that livestock totals in 1971–2 were 12.9 million cattle, 10.9 million sheep, 7.8 million goats, and 2.5 million camels.[16] FAO estimates are somewhat higher than these figures.

Development of the livestock sector in the Sudan is a multi-faceted project. Questions of land use, preservation of social patterns, and availability of surplus manpower are closely tied together with the issue of livestock raising. Cattle owners and herders in the Sudan are bound by tradition, and keep their animals for social and cultural reasons as well as to attain certain economic goals.

The productive system in animal husbandry differs from that in cultivation of seasonal crops in that pastoralists are always faced with investment decisions which can be kept segregated from monetary institutions. In the growing of seasonal crops farmers depend on markets organised on a cash (monetary) basis, and also generally satisfy seasonal capital needs in the organised financial markets.

Cattle raising is an important economic activity in the Sudan. The short-horned zebus with their pronounced humps and neck dewlaps dominate the cattle herds in the northern two-thirds of the country. These animals are able to withstand higher temperature climate. The Kewana variety zebus are found in the south between the White and Blue Nile. These animals range in colour from white to grey. In areas of the Sudan below 10 degrees north latitude native cattle – semi-zebu or Sanga – are found. They tend to have longer horns and a smaller hump than those found in the north. Their meat tends to be of better quality.

In addition to cattle, sheep and goats, camels are of considerable economic importance in the Sudan. They are used for milking, as a means of transportation, and a source of meat. Most are of the one hump or Arabian variety. They are valuable since they can stand the regions of arid conditions. In 1974–5 their value increased from £S.50 to £S.300, in part because of the increased demand in Libya. The Rashaidi variety is rare, bred by the tribe of the same name in the Kassala area. This variety is short-legged, and used more for riding and even racing.

In the traditional sectors of the Sudan land is communal, and cultivators and cattle owners enjoy the right of land use on a joint basis. However, they have no rights to engage in transactions involving sale or lease of the land they use. Therefore, ownership and accumulation of livestock provides the individual herdsman with a certain status, and provides security in case of crop failure. In the context of a tradition-bound non-monetary economy certain institutions evolved which enhanced the attractiveness of this form of investment. Transfer of cattle legitimised marriages, damages were settled by payment of cattle, and status and rank accrued to those able to provide animals for offering at certain rituals. As a result, livestock ownership took on high importance, and there developed a strong preference for the pastoral way of life.[17] The major constraint to herd size is the number of members in the household, and even this can be overcome by taking on additional herders. Consequently, the animal population has grown in the Sudan at a rapid pace, leading to the problems of overgrazing and declining capacity to pasture herds.

The environmental basis of animal husbandry varies from one region of the Sudan to the next. In the following we discuss four regions which account for the greater part of livestock raising in the Sudan. These comprise (1) Equatoria Province, (2) the southern clay plains of Bahr el Ghazal and Upper Nile, (3) the western savannah, and (4) the eastern region of the Sudan.

1. A large part of Equatoria Province is unsuited for livestock raising due to the presence of tsetse fly. In the eastern section the hill peasants keep cattle. This supplements their incomes, which are based on cultivation. In the Kapoeta plains the Toposa tribe has developed social patterns of a pastoral nature. Cultivation of the soil is regarded as the work of women. Clothing is produced from animal hides, and only the women participate in the growing of grain and other cultivated foods. The Toposa is a virtually cashless society, and this is reflected in a low volume of cattle sales. While Toposa cattle are well bred for beef content they are not easily marketed due to lack of disease control. The economic well-being of the Toposa would be improved given the extension of veterinary services and resulting improvement in marketability of cattle.

2. The Dinka and Nuer are dominant pastoral groups in the southern areas of Bahr el Ghazal and Upper Nile. Approximately two million people live in this flat terrain. Considerable migration of people and cattle becomes necessary due to the unpalatable nature of clay soil grasses in the dry season and need for water for cattle. The Dinka drive their cattle into the lower (swampy) areas after the flood waters recede and let their animals feed on the fresh grass. As the waters rise during the next flood they retire with their cattle to the higher ground. While the milk yield of cattle in this region is low, these animals are able to tolerate the more difficult environment and produce relatively good beef. While the population in this region is gradually shifting toward sedentary agriculture, the total cattle population of the three southern provinces remains quite high (4–5 million).

3. The western savannah area is inhabited by the Baggara cattle herders, a mixture of camel owning tribes and a smaller number of cultivators. Considerable environmental constraints apply in this part of the Sudan due to climate and soil conditions. There is considerable variation in rainfall with the northernmost belt receiving minimal (100 mm.) rainfall and the southernmost belt being more generously supplied (800 mm.). In the rainy season of July–September cattle herders move north, reversing direction as the dry season progresses. These seasonal movements involve distances of up to 300–400 km. While at one time the Baggara Arabs were purely nomadic, various factors including population growth and limited pasture area have provided strong incentives for shifting to sedentary cultivation. Less than 10 per cent of the Baggara in southern Darfur are true nomads (i.e., take no part in cultivation at

all). The wealthier Baggara continue to invest in livestock due to lack of alternative investment opportunities. Due to the fact that the cattle thrive under a migratory pattern, herdsmen with sufficient livestock to provide a satisfactory income tend to keep their cattle on the move. Baggara herders tend to respond more readily to market prices than other cattle-raising groups (the Nilotes), and often have a high percentage of take-off from their herds.

In the western savannah cattle marketing is carried out by special traders referred to as the 'Jellaba'. These traders service a vast area over which are scattered numerous small buyers and sellers. These buyers and sellers produce a variety of goods for sale, and in turn purchase a long list of consumer goods including sugar, tea, salt, cloth, and household needs. Due to the wide areas covered, and difficulties of communications, the Jellaba delegate the buying function to agents called 'Wakils'. These local agents purchase cattle when conditions are propitious. The Jellaba merchant delegates a certain amount of authority to the agent, depending on the trust he places in his ability and integrity. Cattle brought to market are sold in an auction-type arrangement in which the 'Sibaba' or middleman may play an important role. The Sibaba buys a few animals at a time from producers and sells the lot to a merchant. The service of the Sibaba is to facilitate transactions in a market which at times operates in a lethargic fashion. For example, on a busy day several hundred cattle may be brought to the market, but sellers are always suspicious of market manipulations by the Jellaba and may dicker endlessly. The Sibaba fill a void in the market and thereby facilitate the distribution process. Hopefully, the private enterprise aspect of cattle marketing will be given free rein to develop further and therefore play an important role in the modernisation of western Sudan.

Cattle in the eastern region of the Sudan are mainly milk animals. Given expansion of irrigated agriculture and mechanised farming, grazing areas available for use by traditional herdsmen have become restricted. Farm tenants in these areas often invest surplus income in livestock, or keep animals in the migratory herds of relatives.

E FORESTRY

1 *Forest Policy and Administration*

The forests of the Sudan represent an important but as yet largely untapped resource. The Five Year Plan of Economic and Social Development (1970–5) included twelve projects for forestry development with a total cost of £S.1.43 million covering plantations (34 per cent), timber production (28 per cent), gum arabic production (22 per cent), reservations and soil conservation (13 per cent), and administration (3 per cent). The Forest Reserve Estate of the Sudan presently stands at 1.5 million hectares, representing 0.4 per cent of the total land area of the nation. National parks and wildlife reserves are administered by the Game and Wildlife Administration. Three national parks and fifteen game reserves encompassing a total area of 5.4 million hectares are managed under the provisions of the Wild Animals Ordinance.

National forest policy in the Sudan is regulated by the Central and Provincial Forest Ordinances.[18] Forest policy and administration was made more decentralised and a greater degree of autonomy was extended to the Provinces in the People's Local Government Ordinance of 1971. Main objectives of forest policy are the regulation of cutting and the assurance of regeneration. With these objectives in mind the Sudan has established two classes of forest reserves, central reserves administered by the Forest Department, and provincial reserves administered by local government authorities. In addition the government of the Sudan has levied royalties on all forest production originating from unreserved forests.

Land ownership and tenure in forested areas follow a variety of patterns. Land inside forest reserves (central or provincial) is declared government land. While very little land can be regarded as privately owned, there are important exceptions. This includes the irrigated plantations of the Sudan Gezira. In addition stands of *acacia senegal* in western Sudan, also known as the Gum Gardens, are privately owned.

The total area of forest plantations is approximately 100,000 hectares, of which 5 per cent consists of exotic species, e.g. *tectona grandis*. The main indigenous species include *acacia nilotica*, *acacia senegal*, *khaya senegalensis*, and *eucalyptus microthaca*. The latter is the main species for irrigated plantations.

2 *Forest Industries*

Numerous industries have developed due to the existence of extensive forest resources in the Sudan. These include sawmilling, charcoal, gum arabic, and wood-based products. Most of the timber in the Sudan is hardwood, although a number of softwood (eucalyptus) species are grown.

All sawmills are government-owned and are operated by the Forest Department.[19] Five groups of sawmills located in the southern half of the country service the Sudan. Four sawmills constitute the Blue Nile group. These mills process *acacia nilotica*, which is used for railway sleepers, construction timber, furniture, roofing, charcoal, and tanning. The Kassala sawmill processes *palanitis egyptica*, which is used for school furniture and home furniture. In Southern Darfur the sawmill processes *acacia alvida* and *sclerocarya*, which is used for furniture. The Wau group of sawmills process mahogany (*khaya senegalensis* or red, and *khaya granfoglia* or light red) which is used in furniture. Also, the Wau sawmills process Vuba which is used in railway sleepers, construction and furniture. Finally, the Equatoria sawmills process Vuba.

The charcoal industry is entirely run by the private sector, under the supervision of the Forestry staff. The Sudanese gum arabic industry supplies 75–85 per cent of the world market demand and gum represents an important export commodity. There are two match factories in the Sudan and one particle board factory in the private sector. Particle board can be cut within five years after planting but better production results from an eight-year growth cycle. The Khartoum factory has capacity to produce 15,000 cubic metres per anum. Several companies have explored the possibility of pulp and paper production, and there are excellent opportunities for plywood manufacture in the future. In future the government hopes to develop export markets for veneer, plywood and pulp. Transport costs represent a problem where exporting is concerned. In the past Sudan has exported small amounts of forest products to neighbouring countries.

In 1975 productive capacity of the Sudan was 154,000 cubic metres of timber per year. The average value (after sawmill) of this timber was £S.40 per cubic metre, yielding an annual value of £S.6,160,000 in sawmill production. Additional sawmills are planned for Southern Kordofan and Southern Darfur. The Forest Department is introducing cyprus and pines as a local softwood in the high elevation areas of Darfur and Equatoria. The forest activities of the Sudan are programmed to the year 2000 and beyond so far as cutting and planting are concerned. Plans are to put down one million acres of gum arabic in the north-west.

In 1975 the Forestry Department had a manpower staff of nearly 6000 plus an additional seasonal labour force of one million man-days. The manpower staff consisted of over 5200 forest labourers, 181 forest rangers (with a two-year college training), 57 rangers, 239 forest overseers, 35 university graduates, and 180 clerical and accounting workers.

3. *Forest Resources of the Southern Region*

Approximately 80 per cent of the Sudan's forestry resources is concentrated in the southern region, primarily in Equatoria and Bahr el Ghazal Provinces. Almost the entire area of Bahr el Ghazal Province is covered with high rainfall savannah woodland. This is also true of Equatoria Province, except for the flood region of Torit-Kapoeta. It has been estimated that the total volume of standing timber of useful species may be in the order of 1,220,000 cubic metres. Assuming that these forests are a wasting asset and ignoring growth, this volume could maintain present cutting levels for over sixty years. If an annual growth of 2 per cent was achieved present levels of production could be maintained indefinitely.[20]

The Sudan currently is a net importer of timber. Forecasts indicate that 80 per cent of requirements will continue to be imported, due to lack of appropriate quantities of locally available timber. In future emphasis should shift to faster-growing hardwoods, and softwoods. An estimate of softwood timber demand for the year 2010 suggests a figure of 116,000 cubic metres. Also, attention will have to be given to the establishment of fuelwood plantations in close proximity to the major towns and adjacent to densely populated areas.

5 Transport, Power and Industry

A TRANSPORTATION

Proponents of economic development often search for a single strategic souce of economic growth. Important candidates include saving, capital formation, entrepreneurial activity and infrastructure. Transportation must rank high in such evaluations. Efficient, low-cost transportation broadens the market area, facilitates export of agricultural products, and lowers the real cost of necessary imports. Even in developed nations investment in transportation facilities constitutes an important activity representing 10–12 per cent of gross domestic investment.

1 *Transport and Economic Development*

In a country such as the Sudan, construction of a highway or extension of a railway line across a nomadic region will impose vast changes on the tradition-bound community. Money will replace barter, commercial agriculture will replace subsistence agriculture, and the pump will replace the *sagia*. An extended market area will bring specialisation and division of labour, and hopefully will contribute to increased productivity. In a country of low population density such as the Sudan the acquisition of new social and economic habits will be spurred on by transportation improvements that widen markets and link together formerly semi-isolated settlements.

Transport development generates forces that ultimately impact industrial development. This is because a nomadic society ordinarily must pass through an agricultural stage of economic growth before industry takes firm root. An efficient and commercially oriented agricultural sector is in most cases a necessary step in the evolution from nomadism to industrialisation.

The role of transportation in this process is evident in the progress thus far achieved in the Sudan during the twentieth century. Widespread use of tractors, pump irrigation and insecticides in the Gezira and Nuba Mountain region, the development of canning factory activities in Kerima and Wau, the successful milk and onion dehydration factories in Babanussa and Kassala are examples of this pattern of development.

Transportation can play an important role in decentralising economic and political development. For the most part developing countries such as the Sudan have not succeeded in decentralizing industrial development. In the Sudan lack of success in diffusing industrial development has brought additional problems such as urban congestion, widening regional disparities in income levels and standard of living, and simultaneous labour shortages and unemployment in various corners of the country. An important challenge in future development policy formulation and transportation planning in the Sudan will be to provide more balanced economic development and industrial progress in all regions of the country.

2 *Present Status of Transportation System*

The transport system of the Sudan consists of a network of 4757 kilometres of single-track railway, 3500 kilometres of river steamship and barge services, and approximately 18,000 kilometres of road and track. The Sudan has twenty all-weather airfields plus the international airport at Khartoum. A single harbour facility at Port Sudan provides access to ocean shipping through the Red Sea. In 1975–6 the final stages of construction were taking place for an oil pipeline between Port Sudan and Khartoum.

In 1975 the transport system in the Sudan relied mainly on the government-owned railway. The road and highway system is not well developed, with more than 75 per cent of roads impassable in the wet and rainy seasons. As recently as 1968 there were only 250 miles of hard-surfaced roads outside the towns and cities.[1] As of 1975 there were still less than 300 miles of hard-surfaced (bitumenised) roads in the Sudan.[2]

The Sudan ranks low among African countries in motor vehicle registrations, with a total of 52,400 vehicles of all types in 1973. Growth in automobile and truck ownership has increased public demand for road improvements. In 1973 less than 2 per cent of the 18,000 km of roads and tracks was paved, with another 13 per cent enjoying gravel surfacing. In the wet seasons (August–October) a special permit is required. Otherwise roads are closed to motor vehicle use. The road between Khartoum and Wad Medani was macadamised in the mid-1960s.

With the lack of development of well-paved roads, and with roads and river transport serving largely as feeders to the rail system rather than offering alternatives to it, the railway is by far the most important means of transport on trunk routes. Railway capacity has been expanded to a point where it can be considered adequate. Nevertheless, the railways suffer from inefficient operations and serve as a major constraint to the expansion of the economy as a whole. In the late 1960s the railroad was carrying 80 per cent of freight traffic, and over 95 per cent of exports.

The Sudan railway encompasses the longest line in Africa. The Port Sudan–Nyala–Wau line is one of six principal penetration routes in Africa south of the Sahara. The only missing links in the Capetown to Cairo rail connection are largely in Sudanese territory. These include the Wau–Uganda connection and the Wadi Halfa and Aswan extension.[3] River transport is an important adjunct to rail transport in the Sudan. The Nile is navigable north from Khartoum into Egypt, and the White Nile and Bahr-el-Gazal are navigable connecting many towns in central Sudan. River steamers provide service south from Khartoum into Equatoria Province. Over 1600 km of riverways are navigable. Kosti on the White Nile is used as a freight transfer point between rail and river modes of transport.

Inland waterways play a vital role in fulfilling the southern regions transport requirements. The river link between Kosti and Juba is presently serviced only to one-third of the potential demand for cargo transport, leaving wide scope for increased investment in river transport services.[4]

Air transport in the Sudan is in the early stages of development. Daily flights connect the major cities in the Sudan, providing passenger and air freight services. International air transport services are provided by Sudan Airways, with regularly scheduled flights linking Khartoum with Cairo, Athens, Beirut, Rome, London, Addis Ababa, Kampala, Nairobi, and Jeddah. In 1973 over 130,000 passengers were carried on the international routes, and domestic flights served an additional 91,000 passengers.[5] In 1975–6 Sudan Airways was in the process of adding two Boeing 737s to its jetfleet, which already included several Boeing 707s.

3. *Railway Development and Policy*

Few countries in the world still rely so heavily on their railway as the Sudan. While railway freight capacity appears adequate, inefficient operations impose a major constraint on expansion of the economy. The government-owned rail system is one of the main sources of employment in the Sudan, with over 36,000 employees, of whom 4700 are classified as skilled (including management, technical, and office workers). In 1975 the lowest-paid rail workers enjoyed a minimum wage of £S.15 monthly. A strong labour union presents a real problem to the government, inasmuch as it is difficult to achieve service efficiencies and balance the operating budget of the Sudan Railway Corporation.

The railway system in the Sudan (Map 5-1, below) has its origins in the 1870s when the British army led by General Kitchener constructed a rail link between Wadi-Halfa and Saras at the northern border. Major construction projects were completed in 1899 (linking Wadi-Halfa and Khartoum), 1909 (linking Khartoum to Sennar on the Blue Nine and Kosti on the White Nile), 1912 (Kosti to El Obeid), 1924 (crossing the Sennar Dam on the Blue Nile and extending the Kassala line to Port Sudan). In 1954 a Sennar–Roseires Dam connection of 143 miles was completed. In the years since World War II several World Bank loans financed further rail line extensions. In 1958 a loan of $39 million facilitated construction of a railway line to Nyala in the southwest. In 1961 an extension was built linking Wau in the south to the Nyala line.

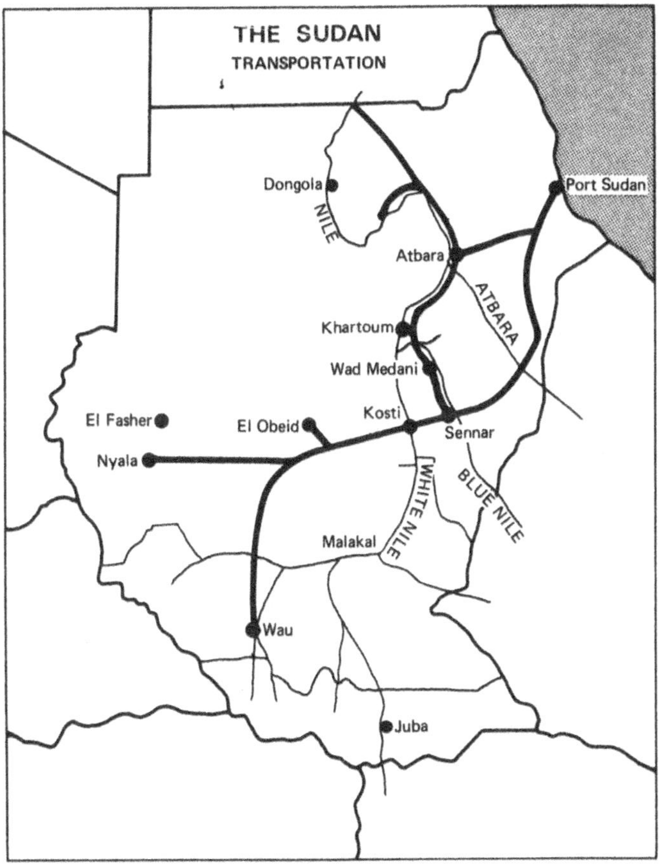

MAP 5-1

Additional World Bank loans in 1965 and 1973 for railway improvements, and a 1972 loan for highway maintenance brought World Bank transport sector loans in the Sudan to a total of $101 million.

The Khartoum to Port Sudan line is the most heavily used in terms of freight traffic, representing 17 per cent of the networks right of way but 60 per cent of freight traffic. This line bears the burden of transporting Sudan's exports and imports to and from

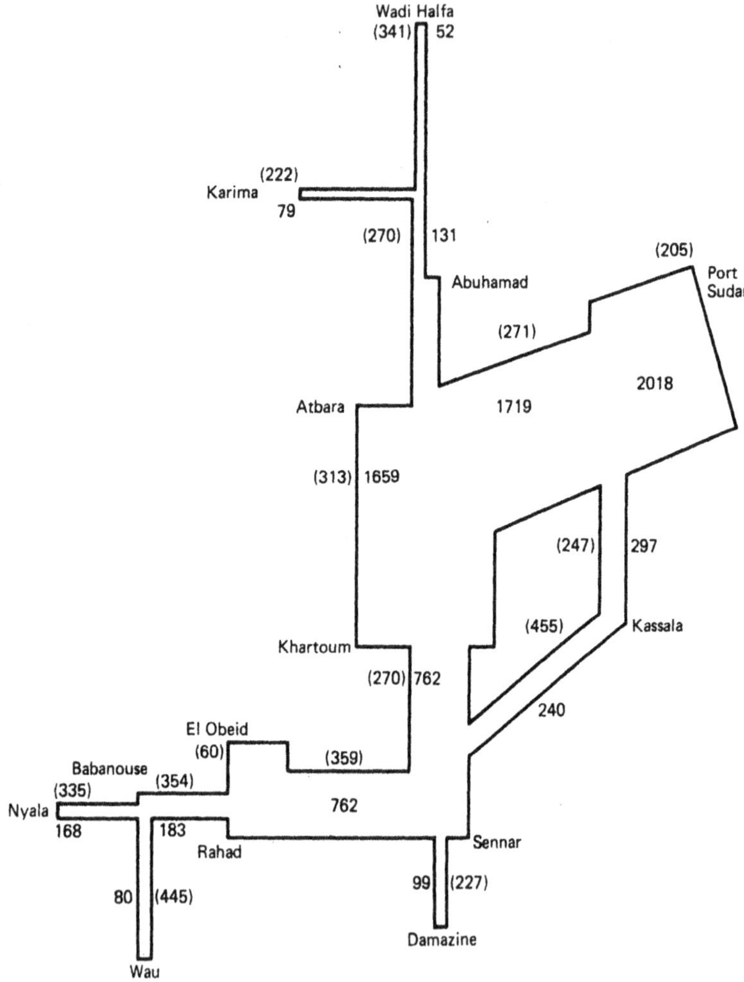

DIAGRAM 5-1 Traffic Density, Sudan Railways, 1973–4

Note Distance in kilometres between points is indicated in brackets. Other figure reflects net tons ('000s).

SOURCE Sudan Railways Corporation, *Annual Report 1973–4*, p. 16.

Port Sudan. As can be visualised from Diagram 5-1, depicting traffic density on the Sudan railway system, the Khartoum–Atbara–Port Sudan route carries more than twice the tonnage carried by the next highest route (El Obeid–Sennar). During the 1960s the railway suffered from use of obsolescent equipment and inefficient operations, in part due to the priority given to extension of lines to outlying areas. Operating problems included track washouts during rainy season, poor maintenance of equipment, inability to operate trains on schedule, overcrowded passenger cars and consequent need for riders to sit on the roof of cars, and inability to ship some agricultural exports for lack of capacity at peak season.

Close to three-fourths of railway revenues is derived from freight (Table 5-1). Competition from the Sudan Airlines in recent years has pulled away passenger traffic and some of the higher-value and more profitable freight business from the railways.

TABLE 5-1 Gross Revenues of Sudan Railway System 1973–4

	£S. m.
Passenger	3.7
Freight	
Merchandise	14.9
Livestock	0.2
Mail, parcel and baggage	0.7
Miscellaneous	0.8
Total	20.3

SOURCE Sudan Railways, *Annual Report*, 1973–4.

One cause of the difficulty that currently faces the Sudan transport system is the policy under the British-Egyptian Condominium of providing a monopoly status to the railway in the overall development of Sudan's transportation system. This policy was openly advocated in the 1930s, and can be rationalised as necessary at that time in light of the relatively low population density in many regions of the Sudan, other than the central area (Khartoum–Gezira–Sennar), and in view of the limited amounts of development capital available for infrastructure investment at that time.[6]

In recent years government policy has turned in favour of providing alternative and competing modes of transport in the Sudan. As a result the government initiated an oil pipeline project to ease the pressure on the rail link to the sea. The pipeline from Port Sudan to Khartoum should relieve the railway of operating pressures.

A second alternative to rail transport in the important Khartoum–Port Sudan corridor would be provided by construction of a tarred road. This would link Khartoum with Port Sudan via Wad Medani and Kassala. A 187-km section of this road has been tarred for a number of years. A Chinese construction group is extending this route by 227 km to Gedaref including a bridge crossing over the Blue Nile at Wad Medani. A contract has been signed with an Italian engineering company to work on a 350 km stretch from Kassala to Haiya. The final 206-km section of this road (Haiya to Port Sudan) is being financed by a donation from the government of Abu Dhabi. It is expected that this road will be open to traffic in 1976–7.

The new competition that the railway system will face should have a leavening effect on the efficiency of operations in the Sudan Railway Corporation which in turn could result in important contributions to the total economy. Moreover, at peak demand periods exports will have an alternative mode of carriage to Port Sudan. Also, the railway system will be less burdened with the need to transport oil to the interior section of the country.

4 *Improvements for the Future*

Transportation and communications continue to be the largest obstacles toward realisation of Sudan's economic potential. In 1975–6 the government allocated one-fifth of its budget to improve transport and communications services. In 1975 the government negotiated to secure a West German investment to set up local and regional television facilities throughout most regions of the Sudan. In the same year a Norwegian investment was arranged to purchase transport equipment (river vessels) to service the Kosti–South Juba route. Norway has indicated an interest in investing in a road construction project linking the southern Sudan with Uganda.

Air transport is likely to play an increasingly important role in the future. The World Bank is financing a study by a British firm for construction of more modern airport facilities in Port Sudan, Malakal and Wau. The Wau airport improvement is needed to develop a capability for shipment of fruit and other locally produced perishables to markets. An airport extension and cargo liners will be needed. Two Boeing 737s are scheduled for addition to Sudan Airways, one having been delivered in 1975 for the daily flight to Juba.

Transport difficulties in the southern region have prompted the development of a plan to construct a canal in the southern swamp (Sud) between Malakal and Juba. In August 1975 an accord was reached between the Sudan and Egypt for construction of the $175 million Jonglei Canal, whereby Sudan provides assurances that the flow of Nile waters to the Aswan Dam will not be interrupted. The 174-mile canal will be 131 feet wide and 13 feet deep, and will take at least four years to complete.

Reopening of the Suez Canal in 1975 has revitalised Port Sudan, and the capacity of the port is being increased to cope with the growth in harbour traffic. Congestion at Port Sudan is reflected in a shortage of berthing facilities, inadequate marine equipment, and inability of the railway and road system to cope with a heavy inflow of imported goods. Construction of a second Red Sea port at Suakin is being considered.

5 *Critique of Transport*

Transport sector planning in the Sudan suffers from the deficiencies that might be expected in a developing country, namely inadequate information and data on which to formulate estimates and plans, and institutionalised patterns of behaviour and operations. The latter problem area includes subsidised railway freight rates and railway union pressures relative to work standards. In the Sudan rail freight traffic subsidises passenger traffic and Khartoum–Port Sudan traffic subsidises the rest of the network. Subsidised transport is politically popular but inefficient. It can lead to improper use of transport facilities and/or selection of improper modes of transport. Subsidised rates can prevent competition between alternative modes of transportation, and can encourage poor location of industry. A proper rate structure could remove such problems as inadequate cash flow and artificially inflated demand for transport services.[7]

Transport investment requires forecasts and data inputs. Data inputs for traffic forecasts require inputs and outputs of population, industry, agriculture, and mining converted into traffic volumes, and then allocated to the least-cost mode of transport. The data base in the Sudan is in an emerging state of development.[8]

The Sudan has engaged specialist consultants to undertake traffic forecasts and develop a transport-oriented macro-model of the economy. ADAR Corporation produced such a model in 1974, in which key sectors and traffic flows were identified. The transport sector was broken down into modes, and inter-regional flows of twelve relatively homogeneous regions were assigned to the various modes on a preference order basis for five classes of goods and two classes of passenger traffic.[9] The traffic demand for each mode was compared with the supply and a gap identification procedure was followed which indicated areas of investment requirements for increasing capacity, replacement and modernisation. The next step was to assign priorities to these investments for the entire sector given a certain composite scenario of the economy in 1985. While the ADAR model is a useful planning tool, it has definite limitations when it comes to investment appraisal. Unfortunately, the model has been applied over-enthusiastically and a large number of investment projects have been subjected to prioritisation procedures which can be considered arbitrary due to use of implicit weightings. Futher criticism of the model hinges on transport cost information which seems to lack accuracy, and a danger that priorities will become institutionalised in the planning structure.

B POWER

As an emerging country with an extremely narrow base of manufacturing industry, the Sudan produces and consumes a comparatively small amount of energy. In 1974 it was reported that public use of electricity was roughly 40 kWh per head of population. The growth in use of electric power has averaged 16 per cent per annum, indicating a doubling of production every four years.

Early development of electric power generating capacity in the Sudan focused on completion of the Sennar Dam in the 1920s, and the Roseires Dam in the 1960s. While hydroelectric power accounts for the largest amount of electric generating capacity, growth has been furthered by installation of thermal power plants.

The Sudan is fortunate in possessing a large potential for hydroelectric power. Hydroelectric generation accounts for over 60 per cent of total output, and development plans call for more intensive use of Nile River potential. It can be seen in Table 5-2 that the estimated potential of hydroelectric power is over three times as large as total current production.

The demand for electric power in the Sudan is associated with the following major uses: (1) the agricultural irrigation schemes – in Khartoum and Blue Nile Provinces all of the agricultural pump schemes are operated by electricity; (2) growth of urbanisation in electricity use is increasing rapidly for street lighting, domestic appliances (including air-conditioners), and offices and commercial buildings; (3) development of manufacturing industry – All industrial areas in the large towns are served with electric power.

It has been established that industry is the main consumer of electric power in the major load centres. In the northern area centred at Atbara industrial use represents 80 per cent of total electric power consumption. In the Khartoum and Blue Nile Provinces industrial use accounts for 40–50 per cent of the total.[10]

Past and future development of electric generating capacity requires overcoming numerous problems and obstacles, some of which are peculiar to the Sudan and others which tend to be intrinsic to the field of power development. One problem is associated with the physical features of the major river system. The

TABLE 5-2 Electric Power Generating Capacity in the Sudan, Actual and Potential, 1974

Location	*Actual power (kW)*	*Potential hydro-power*
Port Sudan	7,895	
Dongola	245	
Atbara	10,000	
Khartoum	51,000	
Khartoum	85,000	
Shendi	945	
Sabaloka		108,000
Kashm el Girba	12,600	13,000
Jebel Aulia		50,000
Medani	9,800	
Sennar	15	30,000
Kassala	3,500	
Roseires	90,000	210,000
Durim	1,020	
Obeid	1,876	
Umn Rawaba	1,165	
Fasher	500	
Nyala	1,884	
Malakal	1,000	
Wau	930	
Juba	1,000	
Nimula-Juba		20,000
4th Cataract		300,000
5th Cataract		175,000
Total	280,375	906,000

SOURCE 'Energy in the Sudan', *African Development*, January 1976.

Nile and its main tributaries are wide rivers, with low heads. This necessitates large and expensive dams, large-size and slow-water turbines, and high capital costs.

A second problem is associated with the fact that nearly all the major factories in the Sudan have had their own independent power supplies installed at the time of plant construction. This applies to factories located in areas supplied by public power as well as factories located in outlying areas.[11] In such cases the cost of the piggyback power station may be one-fifth of the total factory cost. More important, the operating costs of such generating plants are considerably higher than for a centrally located large-scale thermal plant.

A third aspect of the problems faced hinges on the strategic considerations involved in making budget estimates where qualitatively different cost combinations will result and where different development paths will be initiated. Costs incurred in expanding electric power capacity include capital and operating costs, transmission and generating equipment costs, and domestic currency and foreign exchange costs. Where capital costs are involved the interest rate applied and the rate of depreciation can affect the cost levels to a considerable degree. This question was raised in the early 1960s when alternative electric power facilities at Roseires, Sennar II, and Sabaloka were being considered. At the time it was pointed out that the higher capital costs at Sabaloka would be in part mitigated by a lower assigned interest charge on capital. Given the lower operating expenses estimated for the Sabaloka facility, the weight of preference could be shifted away from Sennar II and alternative thermal plants. Another consideration would be the high foreign exchange content of costs associated with the Roseires facility. Finally, access to electric power will exert an important conditioning influence on the location of industry as well as the evolving pattern of transportation links between production points and consumer markets.

Generally, the foreign exchange content of capital outlays for a thermal generating plant are high, in the order of 80 per cent. Hydroelectric plants have a relatively lower foreign exchange component, especially where the civil engineering work can be performed by local contractors. Moreover, hydroelectric plants represent annual savings in foreign exchange that otherwise would be spent for imported fuel.

A fourth problem focuses on the influence of electric power on industrial location. The greater part of electric power generating capacity is centralised in the Khartoum–Gezira area. The availability of low-cost power in this region has tended to concentrate industrial development in this sector of the country. If power does not come to industry, industry will come to power. For reasons of inducing industrial dispersion and more balanced regional growth in the Sudan some effort should be made to develop favourable hydroelectric power sites such as exist at the Fourth and Fifth Cataracts. Industrial concentration in the Sudan is beginning to generate high social and economic costs in the way of urban congestion, escalating expenses associated with providing health and water systems in large towns, and preserving large pockets of low-income and low-productivity labour submarkets.

A fifth problem relates to the different levels of electricity demand in different parts of the country. Urban centres face high load factors as contrasted with low load factors in rural areas. As of 1974 over 80 per cent of electric power capacity was concentrated in the Three Towns area and generating facilities directly connected with Greater Khartoum via primary distribution lines. In the past planning has focused on the needs of the Three Towns area, but has tended to hold back development and electrification in other areas of the country. There is as yet no aggregate national demand factor, and the regional areas in the country largely serve one or two town centres at the expense of potential rural users. In future it will be necessary to assign each region a growth in demand more closely corresponding to population, employment, and industrial potential. In this context it will become necessary to provide more complete transmission line connections between supply and demand points.

A sixth problem focuses on the need to import and transport fuel oil from Port Sudan to the central part of the country, where the largest concentration of thermal generating capacity exists. This has prompted further consideration of expanding thermal generating facilities at Atbara, Kosti and Port Sudan where shorter haulage of fuel oil and/or reduced rail congestion would follow. Completion of the oil pipeline from Port Sudan to Khartoum will reduce the magnitude of this problem.

C INDUSTRY

1 *Development of Industry*

Developing countries generally look to industrialisation as a solution to chronic problems of poverty and economic dependence. With a predominantly agricultural economy, the Sudan has experienced economic setbacks relating to deterioration in crop yields, and fluctuations in cotton and other staple commodity export prices. Consequently, when independence was attained in 1956 the Sudan adopted a policy aiming at agricultural diversification and industrialisation in key business sectors.

When the Sudan attained independence industrial activity represented a negligible portion of Gross Domestic Product.[12] As a result of policies initiated by the government the contribution of manufacturing increased to approximately 8 per cent of GDP in 1966–8,[13] and to nearly 10 per cent in 1970–2.[14] In a parallel development, the number of workers employed in manufacturing has grown rapidly. In 1956 there were 9505 workers employed in manufacturing. This figure expanded to 13,598 in 1960, and to 19,708 in 1962.[15] As can be seen in Table 5-3, 42,823 workers were employed in manufacturing in 1971.[16]

TABLE 5-3 Manufacturing Industry in the Sudan

	No. of establishments		Total production		Total value added		No. of Labourers		Wages		Net invested capital		Total invested capital	
Type of industry	*No.*	%	*£S.'000*	%	*£S.'000*	%	*No.*	%	*£S.'000*	%	*£S.'000*	%	*£S.'000*	%
1. Food, drinks and tobacco	82	39.2	40,029	48.8	8,931	32.6	15,195	35.5	4,428	34.2	7,277	52.1	40,864	39.8
2. Spinning, weaving, ready-made clothing and leather	32	15.3	18,991	23.2	10,760	39.2	15,787	36.9	4,867	37.6	2,361	16.9	34,382	33.5
3. Wood and wood products inc. furniture	8	3.8	322	0.4	77	0.3	604	1.4	121	0.9	78	0.6	718	0.7
4. Paper, paper products, and printing	12	5.7	2,880	3.5	1,433	5.2	2,291	5.3	613	4.7	300	2.1	4,469	4.4
5. Chemicals, chemical products, petroleum and coal	25	16.8	9,998	11.6	2,844	10.4	3,767	8.8	1,222	9.4	1,880	13.4	10,397	10.1
6. Non-metallic products	12	5.7	3,520	3.0	1,161	4.2	1,763	4.1	570	4.4	935	6.7	8,166	8.0
7. Metallic products	1	0.5	730	1.0	232	0.8	78	0.2	61	0.5	114	0.8	392	0.4
8. Metallic, machinery, and equipment	36	12.5	6,658	8.4	1,997	7.3	3,303	7.7	1,057	8.2	1,035	7.4	3,282	3.2
9. Other manufacturing	1	0.5	64	0.1	8	—	35	0.1	8	0.1	—	—	34	—
10. Total manufacturing industry	209	100	81,892	100	27,451	100	42,823	100	12,947	100	13,980	100	102,704	100

SOURCE Democratic Republic of the Sudan, Ministry of Industry, *Industrial Survey 1970–71.*

Modest industrialisation of the Sudan economy has been achieved because the government recognised that growth in manufacturing would facilitate an increase in national income, and due to the recognition that expanding industry would stabilise foreign exchange earnings and income through import substitution and export promotion. Industrialisation was initiated in the Sudan despite numerous obstacles and handicaps. These included the following:

(*a*) inadequate infrastructure, including roads, electric power, and educational institutions.
(*b*) lack of large internal markets and low purchasing power.
(*c*) scarcity of capital, inadequate savings, and means of accumulation.
(*d*) lack of skilled and technically trained workers, and excess of workers engaged in subsistence agriculture.
(*e*) over-concentration of the economy on cotton growing, and cotton export revenues.
(*f*) widespread application of inefficient methods of production using primitive technology, and rooted in a subsistence sector.

Despite these obstacles to the development of industry, the Sudan possesses immense potential and resources. These include favourable possibilities for developing import substitute branches of industry. Moreover, there are several favourable locations for future development of hydroelectric power production. Completion of the Port Sudan–Khartoum oil pipeline will lower the cost of fuel required for thermal energy. Finally, geological research studies have proved that the Sudan contains significant deposits of mineral resources required for industry, including iron ore, manganese, copper, chromite, granite, mica, tin and gypsum.

A cross-sectional view of the manufacturing sector in the Sudan suggests that this potential has been made use of, at least in part. For example, in 1971 the manufacturing sector consisted of 209 establishments producing over £S.81 million of finished and semi-finished goods (Table 5-3). These establishments employed over 42,000 workers whose gross wage earnings were nearly £S.13 million. The total invested capital in Sudanese manufacturing came to over £S.102 million. These figures must be considered in connection with the near absence of industrial activity in the country fifteen years earlier, the widespread low income and subsistence pattern, and the vast stretches of arid, water-scarce territory which represent a real obstacle to regionally diversified industrial development.

Contrary to popular belief Sudanese industries are not all small-scale. The information contained in Table 5-3 indicates that the average number of workers per establishment in each of the industry sectors represented ranged from 35 to 500. A handful of establishments are of good size even by United States standards. For example the Sudan Cotton Textiles Company (owned by Gulf International Ltd), located in Khartoum, employs over 8000 workers, spread over three shifts per day. The Blue Nile Brewery, which operates a capital-intensive plant, employs over 600 workers.[17]

2 *Government Policy and Planning*

Under the Condominium little or no effort was made by the British to develop industry in the Sudan, although they did establish railway maintenance and carpentry shops at Atbara, and similar facilities for repair and improvements at the Gezira. During this colonial period the Sudan was kept as a market for industrial products and source of raw materials. The British administration did not actively encourage development of modern industry in the form of commodity production for the market place. The development of the transport network that took place (1900–55) tended to promote expanded production of exportable raw materials more than internal commodity exchange. During World War II some impetus was given to manufacturing activity, and in the post-war decade several processing industries developed in oil and soap, cement, shoes and canned meat.

With independence the new government set out to formulate a policy of industrial investment, stressing that the field of industry was to be left to private capital and that no discrimination would be made against foreign enterprises.[18] This declaration of policy was confirmed by enactment of the Approved Enterprises (Concessions) Act. 1956, which represents the first systematic step toward industrial development taken by the Sudan.

The Approved Enterprises Act established criteria for a projects eligibility, which included the following:

(1) Benefits to the public interest. This included effect on national income, number of workers employed, and foreign exchange economies.
(2) Prospects for successful development. This included the marketability of the product, industry competition, and expected profitability.
(3) Must not duplicate existing functions. Present production would be compared with expected growth in demand.
(4) Availability of adequate capital and efficient management.

Upon satisfying the above criteria a determination would be made of how much assistance the project should have. All 'Approved Enterprises' were automatically entitled to relief from business profit tax for a period of two to five years. In addition depreciation could be taken in this period at double the normal rates, and profits up to 5 per cent of capital employed were exempt from taxation. Assistance might be given to Approved Enterprises in one or several of the following forms: reduction of import duties on plant machinery and equipment; reduction of import duties on raw materials; facilities for entry of technicians and other foreign employees; land sites at nominal price; provision of technical and commercial advisory services; assured government purchase order for prescribed period; and protective duties on competitive articles from abroad. The effects of the Act were favourable. Widespread interest was reflected in applications for Approved Enterprise status and the number of industrial enterprises multiplied. Unfortunately the overall results fell short in terms of the country's substantial needs for capital formation.

A second important step taken by the government came in 1961 with ratification of the Industrial Bank of Sudan Act. The Industrial Bank was established to fill a gap in the credit system. It was specially equipped to perform the following functions: providing medium and long-term loans for the establishment and expansion of private industrial enterprises; giving secured guarantees for payment in acquisitions of machinery and material necessary for establishment and expansion of private industrial enterprises; extending management and technical advice; and cooperating with appropriate government institutions to further industrial development. Priority is given to projects that have qualified as Approved Enterprises or that fit into the government development plan.[19]

A third area in which the government has initiated efforts to promote industrial development is in vocational training and worker productivity. A number of centres have been established aimed at training skilled workers, and in demonstrating up-to-date techniques in all areas of government and private enterprise employment. One centre at Khartoum was established in 1958. In 1962 the Federal Republic of Germany offered to establish a training centre, and shortly after UNICEF submitted an offer to establish a second centre. Candidates for these centres are drawn from the intermediate schools and are directed toward careers as 'classified industrial workers'. On graduation the candidates are awarded diplomas recognising their completion of the training programme. In 1966 a management training institute began operating, supported by the International Labour Office of the United Nations. The objectives of the institute are to raise industrial productivity, to train supervisors, and to increase the supply of professionally trained business managers.

In addition to encouraging private industry indirectly by means of concessions and tax relief, the Sudan acted directly by establishing a number of government-owned industries. These included two sugar factories, a tannery, a cardboard factory, an onion dehydration factory, a milk processing plant, and two fruit and vegetable canning factories. Most of these were established after 1960. In 1963 the Industrial Development Corporation (IDC) was established to manage government-owned industries. In addition IDC participates in the financing of new enterprises, examines the possibilities of establishing new industries, and can sell its interest in enterprises to the private sector.

In addition to the above mentioned activities the government has attempted to promote industrial development in the following manner:

(1) Established an Industrial Research Institute (1967) to carry out research and render technical services for business enterprises established in the Sudan.
(2) Revised and improved on the Approved Enterprises Act on several occasions (e.g., the Organisation and Protection of Industrial Investment Act of 1967).
(3) Developed and implemented several economic development plans (discussed in Chapter 8).
(4) Completely revised and modernised the investment incentives code in 1972–4.

3 *Location of Industry*

As a developing country the Sudan provides a typical case of regional industrial concentration. In 1966 it was reported that over 70 per cent of the industrial establishments in the Sudan were concentrated in the Three Towns area.[20] Data reflecting results of a government industrial survey of 1970–1 indicate that the concentration of industry remained largely unchanged in the period 1966–71 (Table 5-4). As we can see from the Table, three provinces (Khartoum, Blue Nile, and Kassala) account for 88 per cent of the establishments, 95 per cent of production, 94 per cent of the labour force, 94 per cent of wages earned, and 92 per cent of the invested capital in manufacturing. The Khartoum area has attracted the major part of industry in the Sudan, despite the fact that other areas are more conveniently situated in terms of electric power and raw materials.

A number of factors help to explain industrial concentration in Khartoum. First, Khartoum has the largest concentration of population. Moreover, population growth is highest in the Three Towns, doubling every decade. Khartoum is the largest market centre. Second, *per capita* income in the Three Towns area is two to three times as high as the national average.[21] High *per capita* income expands the market opportunities in terms of purchasing power. More income is available in the Khartoum area that can be spent on

TABLE 5-4 Geographical Distribution of Manufacturing Industry in the Sudan

	No. of establishments		*Total production*		*Value added*		*No. of labourers*		*Wages*		*Invested capital*	
Province	*No.*	%	*£S.'000*	%	*£S.'000*	%	*No.*	%	*£S.'000*	%	*£S.'000*	%
Khartoum	153	73.2	54,144	66.1	16,885	61.5	27,653	64.6	8,693	67.2	48,451	47.2
Blue Nile	18	8.6	13,319	16.3	5,232	19.1	8,541	19.9	1,850	14.3	24,935	24.3
Kordofan	16	7.7	1,366	1.7	545	2.0	928	2.3	202	1.6	2,661	2.6
Dar Fur	3	1.4	157	0.2	31	0.1	124	0.3	10	0.1	170	0.2
Northern	5	2.4	2,146	2.6	859	3.1	1,140	2.7	379	2.9	4,575	4.4
Kassala	13	6.2	10,398	12.7	3,772	13.7	4,164	9.7	1,691	13.0	20,688	20.4
Bahr El Ghazal	1	0.5	362	0.4	127	0.5	263	0.6	122	5.9	924	0.9
	209	100	81,892	100	27,451	100	42,823	100	12,947	100	102,704	100

SOURCE Democratic Republic of the Sudan, Ministry of Industry, *Industrial Survey 1970–71.*

factory production, and this explains in part why producers locate near Khartoum. A third factor is the availability of government offices and departments in Khartoum, and lack of such facilities in many outlying regions. Fourth, the Khartoum region is the most important training and educational centre in the Sudan, supplying a large pool of skilled and semi-skilled workers. Nearly two-thirds of the industrial labour is concentrated in Khartoum.

Fifth, banking and financial services are concentrated in the Three Towns area. Sixth, other services (medical, recreational) are concentrated in Khartoum. Seventh, communications (telephone, television) are concentrated in the Khartoum region. The telephone plays a vital role in a country such as the Sudan in closing the communications gap in commerce and industry.

Eighth, availability of power has played an important role in concentrating industry around the Khartoum area. Producers that decide to locate their factories in areas where no power facilities exist must invest in small-scale and relatively inefficient generating plants to service factory requirements. Ninth, transportation services are required for industrial expansion. Khartoum is the only area in the Sudan that is adequately serviced by rail, road, river and air transport. Tenth, the concentration of industry tends to breed further concentration. Service industries depend on other industry sectors for their existence. Subsidiary industries such as bottling, packing, and maintenance sell their goods and services to industrial firms. Finally, availability of water is an important factor in industrial location. The Nile and its tributaries are the only reliable source of low-cost water, and this continues to be a limiting factor.

Government policy plays an important role in influencing industrial location. The government has not espoused any clearcut policy with regard to the location of industry in the Sudan.[22] While it may not be feasible to inhibit industrial expansion in the Khartoum area, it would be economically justified to provide incentives toward a more dispersed pattern of industrial development.

Sudanese industries can be divided into two broad categories in connection with the forces that influence location, i.e., market-oriented and raw material oriented. The market-oriented group is the largest, and locates in close proximity to urban markets. Some industry sectors produce weight-gaining commodities and transportation costs influence location. These industries tend to grow where consumer demand is substantial. Also many of these industry sectors are maintenance-oriented. They include beer, alcoholic beverages, soft drinks, printing, textiles, soap, footwear, oil, and confectioneries.

Industries that are attracted to the source of raw materials often are weight-losing. Waste materials generally have low value in consideration of use by other industry sectors. In other cases perishable agricultural crops (fruits, vegetables and milk) deteriorate in quality. These crops ordinarily require processing near the production site. These raw material oriented industries include the cardboard factory at Aroma; the onion dehydration plant at Kassala; the sugar industry at Guneid; the cotton ginneries at Kosti, Sennar, and Hasaheisa; the fruit and vegetable canning industry at Kashm el Girba; the fruit canning plant at Wau; and the milk processing plant at Babanousa.

4 *Recent Industrial Development Plans*

The seven-year plan (1970–7) announced by the government includes ambitious objectives and programmes in the area of industrial development.[23] The plan aims at building a stable industrial base, and at providing all the development services required in the basic production areas. Several priorities have been established, which include:

(1) Self-sufficiency in basic consumption areas, so as to provide 75 per cent of imported consumer goods.
(2) Modernising traditional industries and handicrafts to reduce the shift of population from rural to urban areas.
(3) To make use of local raw materials in industry.
(4) To distribute industries throughout all Sudan, where feasible.

Four programmes have been specified in the seven-year plan. These include a self-sufficiency programme in which the Sudan would attain self-sufficiency in sugar, textiles, wheat flour, (kenaf) sacks, paper, cigarettes, ready-made clothing, and canned fruits. These items account for close to one-fourth of imports of consumer goods. The remaining programmes include development of exports (hides and leather, textiles, canned fruits, sacks, and sugar); to further develop and improve on manpower skills; and to further integrate agricultural and industrial processing sectors.[24]

In connection with this industrial development programme, private sector projects under implementation include 423 enterprises with capital investment plans totalling £S.120 million (Table 5-5). The investment projects include food industries, spinning and weaving, wood and wood products, paper and printing, chemicals, metallic products and electrical equipment, and building materials. Public sector projects under implementation are heavily concentrated in sugar factories, weaving, and a variety of other projects (leather, brewery, foundry, pipeline, and fertilisers). In total 24 separate public sector projects are included in these plans with a total cost of over £S.260 milions (Table 5-6).

TABLE 5-5 Private Sector Projects Under Implementation

Sector and type of production	*No. of enterprises*	*Estimated capacity*	*Capital required (£S.)*	*No. of workers*
A Food industries				
Oil mills	118	1,434,800 tons	19,842,542	3,508
Other food	41		1,918,217	1,891
Ice and ice cream		18,000 tons		
Sweets and biscuits		14,000 tons		
Animal feed		105,000 tons		
Automatic bakeries		3,600 tons		
Fish canning		700 tons		
Jam and fruits		870 tons		
Total	159	1,573,730 tons	21,760,759	5,399
B Spinning and weaving industries				
Spinning and weaving (inc. fraad)	76	200,045,840 metres		
Spinning	9	26,101 tons		
Blankets	4	2,150,000 pieces		
Knitwear	2	4,500,000 pieces		
Robes	4	1,000 tons		
Carpets	2	1,800 pieces		
Ready-made clothes	20	20,000,000 pieces		
Total	117		88,925,436	27,697
C Shoes and leather industries				
Shoes		21,360,470 pairs		
Bags		680,600 pieces		
Total	15		484,130	613
D Wood and wood products				
Furniture	8	565,000 pieces	218,622	573

E Paper and paper products				
Printing and packing materials	4	60,875,000 pieces	321,655	163
F Chemical industries				
Plastic industries	20	6,850 tons	929,450	730
Soap	14	12,000 tons		
Yeast	2	1,000 tons		
Drugs	3	180 tons		
Polish	2	130 tons		
Other chemical products	15	9,200 tons		
Total	56		3,156,350	1,754
G Metallic industries and electric equipment industries				
Refrigerators	2	1,200 pieces		
Water and air coolers	2	1,805 pieces		
Fans	1	1,000 pieces		
Putogas	1	600 pieces		
Radio assembly	4	192,000 pieces		
Electric equipment	2	41,500 pieces		
Tev.	2	11,500 pieces		
Other metallic products	15	3,400 pieces		
Total	29		2,745,603	1,872
H Building materials and glass				
Tiles	21	265,000 sq. metres		
Asbestos pipes	1	9,500 tons		
Other building material	11	136,000 tons		
Glass industries	2	272,000 pieces		
Total	35		2,210,000	1,635
Grand total	423		120,751,905	40,442

SOURCE Ministry of Industry, Khartoum, 1975.

TABLE 5-6 Public Sector Projects Under Implementation

Project	*Location*	*Production capacity*	*Total costs (£S.)*	*Labour*	*Execution data*	*Start of product*
I Sugar factories projects						
1. North West Sennar sugar factory	Blue Nile Province	110,000 tons	22,730,000	5,000	1973–4	December 1975
2. Hager Assabya sugar factory	White Nile Province	110,000 tons	22,730,000	5,000	1974–5	1977
3. Kenana sugar factory	White Nile Province	3000,000 tons	65,000,000	9,000	1976–7	1978
4. Mangala sugar factory	Equatoria Province	50,000 tons	15,000,000	25,000	1975–6	1979
5. Melut sugar factory	Equatoria Province	110,000 tons	28,000,000	5,000	1974–5	1978
II Weaving factories projects						
1. Abu Na'ama Kenaf factory	Blue Nile Province	10 m. sacks + 900 ton hessian	6,300,000	600	1972–3	1975
2. Tonj Kenaf sacks factory	Bahr El Ghazal Prov.	10 m. sacks + 900 ton hessian	6,300,000	600	1974–5	1977
3. Friendship weaving factory	Gezira Province	16 m. sq. metres popular clothes	4,000,000	1,950	1972–3	1975
4. Japanese joint weaving factory	Khartoum Province	12 m. sq. metres + dyeing of 24 m. metres	8,000,000	400	1974	1975
5. Port Sudan spinning factory	Red Sea Province	5000 tons fine spinning for export	10,000,000	600	1974	1976
6. El Hag Abdalla spinning factory	Gezira Province	7000 tons spinning to cover the need of 6 weaving factories	10,000,000	600	1974	1976

7. Nyala weaving factory	Southern Dar Fur Prov.	10 m. metres	3,800,000	433	1974–5	1976
8. Ed Dueim weaving factory	White Nile Province	10 m. metres	3,666,000	300	1974–5	1976
9. Mangala weaving factory	Equatoria Province	10 m. metres	3,666,000	300	1974–5	1976
10. Kosti weaving factory	White Nile Province	10 m. metres	3,666,000	300	1974–5	1976
11. Shendi weaving factory	Nile Province	10 m. metres	3,666,000	300	1974–5	1976
12. Kadogli weaving factory	Southern Kordofan	10 m. metres	3,666,000	300	1974–5	1976
III Leather factories projects						
1. Wad Medani tannery	Gezira Province	9.5 m. sq. metres hides	2,016,000	368	1972–5	1975
2. Malakal tannery	Upper Nile Province	150,000 pieces of reptile skins	828,000	200–300		
3. Khartoum new tannery	Khartoum Province	1,756,850 sq. metres hides	1,320,400	400	1971–2	1974 started prod.
IV Different industries projects						
1. White Nile brewery	Bahr El Ghazal Prov.	120,000 seit litres	5,000,000	250	1973–4	1975
2. Central foundry	Khartoum Province	1500 tons	300,000	100 in stage one	1974	1977 1st. stage prod.
3. Port Sudan–Khartoum pipeline		600,000 metric tons per year	11,000,000		1974	1976
4. Fertiliser factory	Red Sea Province	220,000 tons urea	23,000,000			

SOURCE Ministry of Industry, Khartoum, 1975.

It is anticipated that in future the Middle East oil-exporting countries will display increased interest in investing in Sudanese food processing industries, and other industrial projects. This is due to the close proximity, common religious and language ties, surplus of funds available to the oil-exporting countries, and desire to develop a regional complementarity in industrial development.[25]

5 *Mining*

Thus far the amount of geological work carried out in the Sudan to determine the availability of economically exploitable mineral resources has been limited. Nevertheless, it has been determined that there are economically exploitable mineral deposits in different sectors of the country. It is not yet possible to consider the availability of fuels in the Sudan, although some work has been carried out in the north-west in testing for petroleum deposits. Coal has been discovered in a number of water wells dug in the Nubian hills. Methane gas has been discovered in the process of wildcat drilling. The Sudan is endowed with numerous minerals including copper,[26] salt, manganese, asbestos, and lead. The following briefly considers five minerals whose deposits appear to be of significant quantity for future investment and development potential in the Sudan. These are chromium, clay, graphite, gypsum, and iron.

Chromium deposits have been found in three major deposits, including the Ingessana Hills south of Roseires, Galla en Nahl (Kassala Province), and in the northern Red Sea Hills. The deposits in the Ingessana Hills appear to be the most economical and high grade. Shipments of chromium ore to the United States were initiated in the mid-1960s. In the period 1970-3 chrome ore exports averaged 8200 metric tons annually, contributing over £S.200 thousand annually in export receipts.[27] The largest use of chromium ore is in the metallurgical industries. Also chromite refractory brick is used in lining open-hearth furnace bottoms.

Various types of clay deposits have been located in many parts of the Sudan. Some are deposited in Nile River silts, and others are found in Nubian sedimentary formations (and used for making pipes, tiles, bricks and Chinaware). Large kaolin deposits (used in manufacturing white portland cement, as a filter in paper and paint, white porcelain items, and floor tile) have been found in the Sudan. Ingredients other than kaolin that are needed for the manufacture of white goods (felspar and silica) also are available in the Sudan.

Graphite (black lead) occurrences are found in the Kutum area and in the Nuba Hills. Principal uses in developed countries include foundry facings, lubricants, and crucibles. Graphite shapes are used for electrodes, anodes, bricks, and cylinders. Graphite powder is used in making lubricants, plastics, pigments, and dry cell batteries.

Large deposits of very high-grade gypsum have been found all along the Red Sea coast. Gypsum has many important uses including cement making, as a fertiliser, in the manufacture of ammonium sulphate and sulphuric acid, in glass manufacturing, and in housing construction.

It has been suggested that three phases may be identified in the development and use of gypsum.[28] These are as follows:

Phase 1. Use without manufacture, for cement and fertiliser, and as an export commodity.
Phase 2. Use in production of dehydrated products for building.
Phase 3. Use for manufacture of sulphuric acid and other chemicals.

The Sudan has phased into the first stage of utilisation of gypsum, and appears poised and ready to enter the second and third stages.

Iron ore deposits are located in many areas of the Sudan. Three major findings include the Fodikwan and Sufaya deposits in the Red Sea Hills, Abu Tulu Mountain in Kordofan Province, and the Ironstone Area of Bahr El Ghazal Province. These three findings contain rich ores when compared with lower-grade reserves located (and being exploited) in other countries. The Sudanese Fodikwan Iron Mining Company began selling iron ore to Yugoslav enterprises more than a decade ago.[29] Unfortunately, the location of much of the iron ore found in the Sudan makes its commercial exploitation and use uneconomical. This is especially true of the ores located at Abu Tulu and Ironstone. It is possible that Abu Tulu ore can be converted into pig iron for commercial export.

In his analysis of the best use of iron ore for the Sudan economy Elagib concluded that it may be short-sighted to sell unprocessed iron ore for export, since future generations may find it economical to process ore into iron and steel products. Second, there is a vast difference between the price of iron ore and the partially processed and manufactured material. Finally, export of the highest quality ore may further postpone the time when economically feasible smelting can take place in the Sudan. Preferably, the Sudan should find a means to export the lower-quality iron ore.

6 The Financial System

A OVERVIEW OF FINANCIAL SYSTEM

The financial system of the Sudan must be viewed as a necessary catalytic agent for continued economic progress and social development. The system blends together private and public sector priorities and needs in a balanced manner.

Strategic considerations must be kept in mind when evaluating the role and importance of the financial sector and financial activity. The Sudan is an open economy, and volatile export revenues lend a degree of instability to bank deposits and money incomes generated by exports. Import requirements inflate loan demand as goods in transit are inventoried.

A second strategic consideration is the extent of balanced development that can be achieved through judicious use of credit facilities and scarce foreign exchange. Credit is scarcer in the hinterland than in Khartoum, and economic development priorities must be synchronised with import licences and the foreign exchange budget.

Lack of financial services imposes a serious constraint on savings, investment allocation of loan funds, and attainment of efficient growth of the economy. Financial intermediaries are at the embryonic stage, and a stock exchange has yet to be conceived. All will become necessary if economic advance is to be maintained.

B MONETARY SYSTEM AND GROWTH IN LIQUIDITY

Prior to independence the currency in circulation in the Sudan was the Egyptian pound, which had been established in 1949 at the par value of US$2.8716 to the pound. The Sudanese pound was introduced in 1957, retaining the same par value relative to the US dollar. When the United Kingdom and other important trading partners devalued their currency the Sudanese pound retained its valuation relative to the dollar, thereby achieving an upward revaluation in terms of the devalued currency. In 1976 the par value of the Sudanese pound continued at US$2.8716.

The Sudan is a separate, independent monetary area. A large part of its foreign transactions is settled in British pounds sterling at the external rate, which was US$2.50 in 1975.[1] The Sudan is not part of the sterling area and official reserves are held primarily in foreign exchange. Official reserves totalled $124.3 million at year-end 1974, equivalent to 2.3 months of merchandise imports.

Sudan has entered into bilateral payments agreements with Egypt, the German Democratic Republic, India and Poland.[2] Payments to Egypt for gasoline and Suez Canal dues must be made in convertible currencies. All other payments are settled through the bilateral account. Exchange control is administered by the Bank of Sudan, with responsibility for effecting detailed transactions delegated to the authorised banks.

The money supply and liquid asset holdings of the non-bank public have expanded noticeably in the years since attainment of independence. This is an important achievement, and reflects growth of the banking system, further development of a money-oriented economy, and favourable incentives toward saving and capital formation.

The interrelationship between money, banking, and capital formation is critical to the success or lack of success experienced in a less developed country's overall development. It is difficult to find the extremes of overly tight (financial repression) monetary policy or inflationary development finance in the Sudan. In Table 6-1 we find data pertaining to the growth of money supply narrowly defined as M_1 (currency and demand deposits) and more broadly defined as M_2 (including M_1 plus time and savings deposits), compared with the expansion of GDP from 1956 to the early 1970s. M_1 increased from approximately 10 per cent of GDP in 1956 to nearly 20 per cent of GDP in 1970–2. While time and savings deposits rise sharply from an extremely low base, they represent barely 14 per cent of M_1 in 1972. Consequently, M_2 increased relative to GDP over the 16-year period, rising from 10 per cent to 22 per cent.[3] The increased relative importance of M_1 and M_2 to GDP is to be expected at this stage of development for the Sudan. Moreover, the growth of M_2 relative to GDP should continue as financial savings accumulate in the form of bank deposits. Unfortunately, global inflation overtook the Sudan in the early 1970s (see columns 6 and 7 in Table 6-1) and if unchecked could furnish strong disincentives to the accumulation of financial savings via growth in time and savings deposits.

While the Sudan reflects only the earliest stages of development in its banking institutions and financial markets, there has been a noticeable expansion in liquid asset holdings by the non-bank

TABLE 6-1 Growth of Money Supply, Gross Domestic Product, and Price Level Changes in the Sudan, 1956–72

Year	*Money Supply* Demand deposits plus currency M_1	Time and saving deposits	Total M_2	Gross Domestic Product	Ratio of M_2 to GDP	Wholesale prices (1963 = 100)	Consumer prices (1963 = 100)
	1	2	3	4	5	6	7
1956	30.19	0.45	30.64	300.0	0.102	114.1	79.4
1958	32.32	1.00	33.32	301.2	0.111	103.8	86.6
1960	37.13	2.07	39.20	386.8	0.101	99.4	86.6
1962	52.31	3.64	55.95	456.2	0.123	101.9	95.5
1964	58.09	4.94	63.03	476.8	0.132	108.0	103.9
1966	70.03	8.12	78.15	497.6	0.157	106.6	103.1
1968	78.58	11.80	90.38	583.2	0.176	111.7	103.0
1970	109.58	13.51	123.09	637.6	0.193	126.7	120.7
1972	137.73	20.58	158.31	707.3	0.224	142.8	132.2

Columns 1, 2, 3, and 4 are expressed in £5.m.
SOURCE IMF, *International Financial Statistics*.

private, bank, and government sectors. Total liquidity in the Sudan expanded from £S.66 million in 1954 to £S.372 million in 1974 (Table 6-2). Between 1954 and 1974 total liquidity in the Sudan increased from approximately one-fourth of GDP to four-tenths of GDP.

The three major economic sectors each held a changing percentage of this liquidity, these changes reflecting the ebb and flow of savings, borrowing, and economic activity in the Sudan. In the 1950s the government sector held over half of total liquidity, reflecting a poorly developed post-colonial expatriate banking system, and little accumulation of savings by individuals in the private sector. By the mid-1960s the non-bank sector had increased its share of liquidity to 75–80 per cent of the total A money-based economy had emerged, and financial saving had taken hold as an important aspect of economic activity. The government sector experienced reduced liquidity in the 1960s as it endeavoured to finance much-needed development projects by drawing down cash balances. Commercial bank financing of government capital expenditures increased the share of liquidity held by the banking system.

C BANKING AND CREDIT

The banking system in the Sudan consists of the central bank (Bank of Sudan), five nationalised commercial banks,[4] and three special-

TABLE 6-2 Expansion of Liquidity in the Sudan Financial System, 1954–74

	I *Liquid assets held by non-bank public*						II *Liquid assets held by banking system*			III *Liquid assets held by government*			
	Money supply M_1	*Demand deposits*	*Currency*	*Time saving deposits*	*Post office savings*	*Sub-total*	*Bank reserves*	*Bank claims on govt.*	*Sub-total*	*Deposits in banks*	*Deposits in central bank*	*Sub-total*	*Grand total*
	1	2	3	4	5	6	7	8	9	10	11	12	13
							£S. m.						
1954	27.51	5.38	22.13	0.94	1.09	29.54	1.13	—	1.13	5.80	30.48	36.28	66.95
1960	34.98	14.79	20.19	2.07	2.12	39.17	7.06	—	7.06	13.61	46.74	60.35	106.58
1966	69.50	28.16	41.34	8.12	5.30	82.92	5.22	5.17	10.39	1.23	10.37	11.60	104.91
1968	78.02	31.06	46.96	11.80	6.20	96.02	7.32	5.09	12.41	1.30	14.24	15.54	123.97
1970	108.19	41.37	66.82	13.51	6.93	128.63	4.90	15.74	20.64	2.24	7.63	9.87	159.14
1972	136.11	60.89	75.22	20.58	7.31	164.00	10.68	20.24	30.92	4.82	12.67	17.49	212.41
1974	200.54	92.75	107.69	38.15	13.18	251.87	35.60	23.52	59.12	5.04	56.39	61.43	372.42
							AS % OF TOTAL						
1954	41.0	8.0	33.0	1.5	1.6	44.1	1.7	—	1.7	8.6	45.4	54.1	100.0
1960	33.0	14.0	19.0	1.9	1.9	36.8	6.6	—	6.6	12.7	44.1	56.8	100.0
1966	66.2	26.8	39.4	7.7	5.1	79.0	4.8	4.8	9.6	1.2	10.3	11.5	100.0
1968	62.9	25.0	37.9	9.5	5.1	77.5	5.9	4.1	10.0	1.0	11.5	12.5	100.0
1970	68.0	26.0	42.0	8.5	4.4	80.9	3.0	10.0	13.0	1.3	4.9	6.2	100.0
1972	64.2	28.7	35.5	9.7	3.4	77.3	4.8	9.7	14.5	2.2	6.0	8.2	100.0
1974	54.0	25.1	28.9	10.3	3.4	67.7	9.6	6.3	15.9	1.4	15.1	16.5	100.0

SOURCE IMF, *International Financial Statistics*.

purpose banks. These are the Agricultural Bank, the Industrial Development Bank, and the Estates Bank.

The banking system has experienced dramatic development since the attainment of political independence in 1956. Prior to independence the Sudan banking system possessed all the earmarks of colonial banking. The commercial banks were branches of foreign institutions, there was no central bank, and local currency (in this case Egyptian banknotes) and British coins circulated side by side as legal tender. After independence the Sudan Currency Board was established (1957) to issue the new Sudanese currency. In 1959 the Bank of Sudan Act was passed and in the following year the central bank became one of the first operational central banking institutions in independent Africa. The Bank of Sudan assumed responsibility for administration of foreign exchange and related currency matters including regulation over the issue of notes and coins, development of a sound credit and banking system, and serving as banker and financial adviser to the government.

1 *Commercial Banks*

After nationalisation of the seven existing commercial banks in 1970, the Bank of Sudan Act vested greater powers and responsibilities in the central bank. The commercial banks were converted into limited companies fully owned by the Bank of Sudan, which is considered the competent administrative authority to control and supervise the nationalised banks. In addition, the Bank of Sudan was empowered to exercise direct control over the commercial banks and to issue direct orders to them in cases where this is deemed useful for achieving monetary policy objectives.[5] In 1973 a reorganisation of the banking system took place and the number of banks was reduced from seven to five.

Commercial banks are institutions which attract deposit funds and channel them to borrowers on the basis of economic and social priorities. The commercial banks in the Sudan have been able to attract deposit funds from various sources, whose importance has shifted over the years. At independence government deposits represented the single most important source of deposit funds. Establishment of the central bank in 1960 was followed by a shift of deposits to that institution, so that by 1966 government deposits accounted for less than 3.5 per cent of total commercial bank deposits. The shift of Cotton Marketing Board and similar government agency deposits to the central bank probably will result in a more stable pattern of deposits in commercial banks. Cotton export receipts especially have been a major source of instability in bank earnings and deposits. In the past an important source of deposits has been the expatriate and indigenous business firms operating in

TABLE 6-3 Combined Balance Sheet of Commercial Banks (£S.'000)

	31.12.72	31.12.73
LIABILITIES		
Deposits:		
Government(a)	2,839	2,215
Boards	40	712
Local government	2,055	1,345
Private	81,352	101,538
Bankers:		
Bank of Sudan	6,373	9,273
Other banks	309	827
Foreign Correspondents:		
(a) Scheduled territories	2,482	2,212
Egypt	2,271	2,271
Others	2,278	2,714
(b) Kuwait deposits for the K. S. Co.	—	5,915
Capital	6,361	6,361
Other accounts	20,849	33,082
TOTAL LIABILITIES	127,209	168,465
ASSETS		
Cash (Domestic)	2,693	3,298
Balances with banks:		
Bank of Sudan	7,987	15,201
Other banks	236	231
Treasury bills	15,000	18,250
Foreign correspondents:		
Scheduled territories	386	527
Egypt	—	—
Other	470	3,353
Cash (Foreign)	45	79
Advances, etc.:		
To private borrowers	84,787	98,780
Government securities	5,240	5,240
Other accounts	10,365	23,506
TOTAL ASSETS	127,209	168,465

(a) Including balances of the Agricultural Bank.

SOURCE Bank of Sudan, *Fourteenth Annual Report*, March 1974, p. 56.

the Sudan. In 1973 a new banking control law provided for the establishment of a savings and investments council, the main objectives of which are to encourage thrift, coordinate the operations of the existing savings units, establish new savings units, and formulate policies with regard to the financial and administrative requirements of the banking system.

Examining the overall position of the commercial banking sector nearly two-thirds of deposit sources of funds are derived from private depositors (Table 6-3). Substantial liabilities are due to foreign correspondents, particularly to countries with whom the Sudan has negotiated bilateral payments agreements. In 1973 the external liabilities position of Sudanese commercial banks increased due to a large Kuwaiti loan made to the Sudanese Investment Co. through the commercial banks.[6] On the assets side, advances to borrowers make up nearly two-thirds of commercial bank resources. During 1973 commercial bank holdings of Treasury bills increased by £S.3.3 million, adding to the liquidity position of the banking sector. In February 1973 the Treasury Bill Act was amended, permitting an increase of £S.10 million in commercial bank investments in Treasury bills.

The commercial banks enjoy a high degree of freedom in their loan and investment activities. The only exceptions to this occur when a shortage of foreign exchange takes place due to a crop failure, or when credit ceilings are imposed in connection with an overall programme of economic and financial stabilisation. Commercial bank lending is mainly short-term. In 1973 short-term advances represented 92 per cent of total advances (Table 6-4).

TABLE 6-4 Commercial Bank Advances to Private Borrowers (£S.'000)

	Short-term advances					
	Exports					
	Cotton	*Others*	*Imports retail trade and private professional*	*Others*	*Medium and long-term advances*	*Total advances*
31.12.71	7,835	16,973	11,342	23,785	9,895	69,830
31. 3.72	5,984	19,934	9,942	28,509	9,765	74,134
30. 6.72	2,097	16,198	8,090	33,435	10,659	70,479
30. 9.72	4,245	11,511	8,346	33,825	10,703	68,630
31.12.72	10,816	24,237	7,919	31,224	10,591	84,787
31. 3.73	6,576	29,981	7,672	35,392	10,578	90,199
30. 6.73	12,335	22,088	8,290	39,314	10,786	92,813
30. 9.73	10,060	19,893	9,196	40,727	7,608	87,484
31.12.73	4,869	25,552	9,723	50,712	7,924	98,780

SOURCE Bank of Sudan, *Fourteenth Annual Report*, March 1974, p. 58.

Within the short-term financing category there was a marked shift in the mid-1960s toward working capital loans of industrial enterprises. This emphasis on short-term financing by the commercial banks and lack of long-term lending facilities explains in part why the Sudan government established the three specialised development banks in the period 1959–67 (Agricultural Bank, Industrial Development Bank, and Estates Bank).

Advances made by the commercial banks have exhibited strong growth. In the two-year period reflected in Table 6-4 there was an expansion of over 43 per cent. The quarterly data reflect constant reallocation of bank credit among different borrowing sectors. This results from fluctuations in cotton and other exports, changes in import activity and volume of retail trade, and changes in demand for funds by industrial enterprises. Approximately one-third of bank advances are directly associated with foreign trade activity, indicating the strategic importance of export–import trade to the Sudan economy.

During the calendar year 1973 commercial bank advances to private customers increased by £S.14 million. The largest increase was in advances for financing industrial enterprises (£S.9.2 million), due to an increased volume of activity and rising prices of raw materials. In addition, there was an increase of £S.7.0 million in advances for financing business enterprises, mainly contractors engaged in building and construction. There was a small increase in advances related to imports and trade in imported goods, accounted for largely by higher prices of imported goods. As a result of higher domestic prices advances for trade in locally manufactured goods increased by £S.1.5 million. Advances for financing exports declined by £S.4.7 million (resulting from a substantial decline associated with financing cotton exports and a moderate increase related to financing other exports).

2 *Special Purpose Banks*

Three special-purpose banks play an important role in the Sudan in providing loans in credit sectors where there is an absence of alternative sources of funds. These institutions are described in the discussion which follows.

The Sudanese Estates Bank was established in 1966 and commenced operations in the following year. The objectives of the Bank are to provide financial assistance in the housing sector by means of extending long-term loans to individuals for the purpose of constructing urban dwellings. A housing shortage in the rapidly growing urban centres of the Sudan provided the stimulus for establishing the Estates Bank. The Bank is further charged with the responsibility of undertaking research designed to improve building standards and to promote the use of local materials in the construction industry.

The total paid up capital of the Bank at 30 May, 1973 was £S.3.6 million, all of which was subscribed by the Bank of Sudan. In the four-year period 1969–72 the Bank had made 2863 separate loans with a total value of £S.2,550,000. The Estate Bank Act requires the lending institution to extend 65 per cent of its loans to low-income borrowers, and a further 30 per cent to middle-income borrowers. The interest rates charged by the Estates Bank are 4.5 per cent for low-income loans, 6 per cent for middle-income loans, and 10 per cent for commercial loans.[7]

The Industrial Bank of Sudan was established in 1961 to assist and promote the establishment and modernisation of private industrial enterprises in the Sudan, and to encourage the participation of both internal and external private capital in Sudanese enterprises. At 30 May, 1973 the Industrial Banks paid-up capital was £S.2.8 million, all of which was owned by the Bank of Sudan. The Industrial Bank can finance public sector as well as private sector enterprises in the form of equity and loan investments. The Industrial Bank is authorised to obtain additional funds over and above its paid in capital by borrowing. However, borrowing is limited to three times its own net worth. The Industrial Bank may be expected to play an important role in the Sudan's financial development.

From its inception to 1975 the Industrial Bank extended financial assistance to 156 industrial projects, involving a total investment of close to £S.13 million of which the Bank contributed over £S.6 million. In the two-year period 1971–2 the Industrial Bank extended loan commitments of £S.340,000 and guarantees totalling £S.792,000. These guarantees generally cover the importation of capital equipment under suppliers' credits. The Bank charges interest rates of 8.5 per cent on term loans (up to 6-year maturity) and 9.5 per cent for loans extending beyond 6 years. The rate of interest charged for foreign currency loans also is 9.5 per cent. The Industrial Bank ordinarily levies a guaranty fee of 2 per cent on such credits.

The industrial investment climate has become more favourable in the Sudan since 1970, when a number of private sector establishments were nationalised. As of 1972 approximately 65 per cent of manufacturing assets were owned by private sector establishments, and the government has indicated it intends to rely almost completely on private investment in the manufacturing sector. With passage of several investment development and promotion acts since 1972 domestic and foreign investor interest in the Sudan has picked up. The International Finance Corporation made an investment of US$1.5 million in 1972 to expand operations of a large cotton textile mill in Khartoum. Given the large size of the domestic market, there is considerable scope for setting up manufacturing capacity for import substitution. Moreover, there are numerous opportunities for agro-based industries using local raw materials.[8]

The Industrial Bank of Sudan is the only specialised financial institution in the Sudan catering to the long-term credit requirements of the industrial sector. During periods of economic and financial austerity ceilings on commercial bank credit fixed by the central bank at the insistence of the International Monetary Fund leave the banking sector little opportunity to expand credit, even when banks possess sufficient liquidity. The Industrial Bank is limited in that its maximum loan exposure to any single enterprise cannot exceed 20 per cent of its net worth in the case of a public sector corporation, 15 per cent of its net worth in the case of a partnership, and 10 per cent of its net worth in other cases. Industrial Bank maximum exposure in the *equity* of an enterprise cannot exceed 10 per cent of IBS net worth. Finally, IBS can lend up to a maximum of two-thirds of the total cost of a project.

In 1973 IBS negotiated a US$4 million line of credit with the World Bank. In 1975 IBS was negotiating a second line of credit with the World Bank, and arranging for additional credits with the Arab Development Fund.

The Agricultural Bank of the Sudan began operations in 1959 with authorised capital of £S.7.0 million contributed by the government in instalments. By law the stated policy of the Agricultural Bank is as follows:[9]

(a) that preference is given to small and medium cultivators as well as cooperatives;
(b) that the Bank will take the initiative to increase productivity by supplying improved seeds, insecticides, fertilisers as well as extension services;
(c) that the Bank will help producers in handling and storage of crops, and supply information regarding market conditions.

Farmers are expected to participate with a minimum of 30 per cent of the funds required to create a sense of responsibility and to insure their commitment. The Bank accepts as security for short-term loans movable property and crop guarantees; for medium-term loans and long-term loans real estate security, deeds, shares and other collateral. Land offered as security must be registered as freehold or leased for a sufficient period of time longer than the time of repayment of the loan. The value of security offered in all cases must be 30 per cent more than the amount of loan applied for.

The Agricultural Bank has 13 branch offices, five with sub-branches. Branch managers are authorised to approve loans not exceeding £S.1000 to a single farmer. Larger loans must be approved by Bank headquarters. Repayment of short-term or seasonal loans is normally made in one instalment coinciding with harvest, or by depositing the crop with the Bank. Medium- and long-term loans are repaid in instalments as agreed in the original negotiation. In the period 1966–8 over 30,000 households received new loans from the Bank, and in 1969–70 4460 households received new loans. In 1970 the Bank reported that 13 per cent of loan volume (£S.3 million) was overdue.

3 *Agricultural Credit*

It has been noted that organised banking has a poor record in penetrating the economic hinterland of developing countries, in serving rural areas, and in serving small agricultural borrowers in particular.[10] In the Sudan agricultural credit suffers from deficiencies often encountered in developing countries. These include a lack of modern sector financial institutions to mobilise and channel credit to individual farmers and tenants, the consequent high cost of a predominantly tradition-oriented credit mechanism, and the inability of farmers and tenants to extricate themselves from an inefficient and costly credit system.

Agricultural credit in the Sudan falls into two broad categories, the traditional system of *Shail* and the non-traditional or modern credit system. The modern credit system is made up of the commercial banks, the Agricultural Bank, and quasi-public bodies such as the Sudan Gezira Board (SGB). Many farmers and farmer tenants do not actively seek or have ready access to sources of credit from the modern sector due to a lack of suitable assets to serve as collateral for loans, low risk-bearing capacity and managerial ability, inability to establish effective contact with lending institutions (e.g. through agricultural cooperatives), lack of transport facilities to bring credit into remote areas, latent fear of other (modern) credit systems which they have no familiarity with, and simple defence of traditional methods and value systems.[11]

A necessary solution to the problem of institutional credit (in a large part due to lack of tangible security) is close supervision of farmers by Agricultural Bank branches. This has to be intensified. The full link of financing with processing and marketing currently feasible only in cotton and tobacco (through the Sudan National Tobacco Corporation) needs to be widened to include other products.

The traditional system of agricultural credit is widespread in the Sudan, and associates itself firmly with subsistence farming and tenant farmers in the more advanced irrigated areas such as the Gezira. The *Shail* system extends through the Northern Province,

Kordofan, Southern Blue Nile, Kassala, and White Nile regions. Three basic forms of *Shail* include an advance of seed against a future crop, a middleman service where the moneylender takes over the crop at market price less an amount approximating the interest rate on short-term advances, and an advance of money against future crops. The crops used in *Shail* transactions generally include durable cereals, oil crops, and groundnuts.

Shail operators are not full-time professional moneylenders but are engaged in credit activities as a subsidiary occupation. Their primary occupation may be as (wealthy) farm tenants, village merchants, shaikhs, livestock owners or religious leaders. The *Shail* merchant draws part of his credit resources from a more substantial merchant in a nearby town, who in turn acquires capital from the three towns area.

Shail credit is usually short-term, with the main security provided by the crop which can be visually inspected. Social attitudes permit acceptance of the good faith of the borrower by the *Shail* merchant. Moreover, village life is intimate and closely bound together with marital and blood ties. Third party guarantees apply in the case of young tenants whose uncle or father stand ready to support the relationship. *Shail* is used by farm tenants who require consumer credit as well as producers' advances. A high percentage of Gezira tenants borrow for purchase of family food, to fulfill social obligations and for other purposes.

Farmers using the *Shail* system receive prices for their production which are substantially below current market prices. Prices received by the low-income tenant farmers were found to be lower than those received by high-income farmers, reflecting weaker bargaining power. The *Shail* market price ratio can be used as an indicator of gross profit obtained by *Shail* merchants. The study referred to above reported that gross profits of *Shail* merchants in the Gezira were 47 per cent, 72 per cent, and 65 per cent for loans on dura, wheat, and groundnuts, respectively. By contrast, gross profits of moneylenders in Eastern Kordofan Province were 48 per cent, 50 per cent, and 67 per cent of the harvest value of groundnuts, sesame and gum arabic, respectively.[12] In effect, when a tenant sells his crop forward under *Shail* the price he obtains is less than 50 per cent of the market value of the product. Despite this high cost, the *Shail* system continues. The tenant regards this system as one that readily grants him the funds to meet necessary expenses (food, field planting, and harvesting). *Shail* merchants are flexible regarding repayments, and as a result some tenants are chronically in debt. For them *Shail* has become a way of life.

A solution to the problem of *Shail* will be gradual and will require considerable time. *Shail* and the traditional system of agricultural credit will continue to be important in the Sudan for many years to come. A number of approaches will be necessary to improve agricultural credit and gradually displace the practice of *Shail.* One approach will be to focus on increasing net returns received by tenants. This could be accomplished by providing a larger and more stable supply of farm labour, reducing the cost of agricultural inputs, and improving rotation of crops. Additional approaches should include erection of grain storage facilities (tenants deposit grain in local stores which permit withdrawals against their accounts), improved production through education and training which would raise incomes, extension of cooperative facilities and services, and improved transportation for rural areas.

D THE CENTRAL BANK

The Bank of Sudan was incorporated in 1959 to assume monetary powers previously exercised by the Sudan Currency Board. The Bank acts as financial adviser and banker to the government. In this regard it administers and participates in negotiations for foreign loans and credits to the government, and plays an important role in maintaining relations between the government and the International Monetary Fund. In addition to its role as banker for the government, which is described in a later section of this chapter, the Bank of Sudan also is responsible for control over credit creation in the Sudan, and plays a major role in managing the balance of payments and foreign exchange reserves of the nation. Also, the Bank of Sudan is responsible for issue and control of currency in circulation.

A basic function of the Bank of Sudan is credit control designed to curb inflation and assure equilibrium in the balance of payments. In a relatively open economy such as the Sudan effective credit control necessarily includes supervising the use of credit in foreign trade. This is due to the implications that changes in the balance of payments have for money supply and industrial activity. In this section the concept of credit control concerns itself mainly with the central bank's role in influencing the volume of credit extended by the commercial banks and specialised banks to the private sector. In the following section on government financial policies we further examine the Bank of Sudan's role in providing credit facilities to the central government and government bodies.

The instruments of credit control employed by the Bank of Sudan are principally (1) overall lending limits on individual commercial banks; (2) a maximum ceiling for all categories of commercial bank advances except those intended to finance exports; and (3) limitations on bank advances to finance imports and trade in imported goods.[13] In 1971 restrictions on imports took the form of an increase from 40 to 60 per cent in the margin on letters of credit. Commercial banks may obtain advances from the Bank of Sudan based upon such credits to private customers (against warehoused cotton). This activity is reflected in line 17 in Table 6-5. The credit ceilings imposed on banks are reinforced with statutory limits on

TABLE 6-5 Balance Sheet of the Bank of Sudan (£S.'000)

	31.12.72	31.12.73
LIABILITIES		
1. Notes and coins in circulation	77,909	96,064
Sight Liabilities:		
2. Central government	6,952	4,839
3. Banks: Commerical	8,001	14,115
4. Banks: Specialized	1,618	2,175
5. Boards	218	391
6. Payments agreements	13,728	11,771
7. Others	5,625	6,549
8. Time liabilities	15,825	19,227
9. Capital and reserves	5,033	5,025
10. Other accounts	29,703	29,121
11. TOTAL LIABILITIES	164,612	189,277
ASSETS		
External assets eligible under section 32 of the Bank of Sudan Act:		
12. Foreign notes, cheques and bank balances	3,267	7,904
13. Foreign securities	7,283	7,588
14. Holdings of SDRs	1,841	5,832
15. Other external assets	6	10
16. Payments agreements	664	2,912
Loans and advances:		
17. Commercial banks	7,258	9,229
18. Specialized banks	1,433	844
19. Temporary advances to the government	30,200	8,000
20. Long-term loan to the government under Section (57)	33,800	64,000
21. Advances under section (57A)	49,499	48,890
22. Participation in banks	14,810	16,610
23. Other participations	1	1
24. Non-transferable treasury bills	12,978	12,978
25. Other accounts	1,572	4,479
26. TOTAL ASSETS	164,612	189,277

SOURCE Bank of Sudan, *Fourteenth Annual Report*, March 1974, p. 53.

Bank of Sudan advances to the central government and governmental bodies.

The Bank of Sudan pays particularly close attention to the growth in money supply and to the factors that influence this expansion.[14] Instruments of monetary policy utilised actively by central banks in industrialised countries such as open market operations, changes in reserve requirements, and changes in the discount rate, do not play a role in the Sudan. Credit directives and guidelines for credit allocation are considered to be more suitable for the Sudan economy as well as easier to administer.

In 1973 the stabilisation programme worked out jointly with the International Monetary Fund imposed specific lending limits on the banking system in connection with credits to private and public sector borrowers. At this time overall Bank of Sudan policy was geared toward restricting credit for imports while providing adequate export financing. In the period 1972–3 commercial bank credit facilities to the private sector exceeded the prescribed ceiling by about £S.11 million, due to transport bottlenecks and shipment delays which led to increased financing of goods in transit.

The international financial role of the Bank of Sudan concerns itself with management of foreign exchange reserves (lines 12–15 in Table 6-5) and regulation of the foreign exchange rate. In this connection the central bank administers allocation of import licences, provides foreign exchange allocated under overseas travel allowances of residents, and monitors capital transactions and debt service payments. Finally, the Bank of Sudan participates in the preparation of the national foreign exchange budget by projecting the availability of foreign exchange. In turn the Minister of Finance and National Economy makes allocations for commodity imports. Subsequent to this the Bank of Sudan issues import licences within designated limits.

E GOVERNMENT FINANCIAL POLICY AND TAXATION

Government financial policy plays a key role in the degree of successful performance achieved by the national economy. Given low income levels, shortage of savings, and small base of entrepreneurial activity in the Sudan, a heavy burden falls on the central government budget to achieve multifold objectives. According to a statement included in the central bank *Annual Report* of 1973,

> The main objectives of the ordinary budget are to achieve a surplus in the balance of payments through increased production and exports while maintaining a reasonable level of imports, to achieve a surplus in the budget to help in financing development, to control inflation and to achieve equity in distributing the financial burdens among citizens.[15]

In the period 1969–73 the central government budget fell short of the above stated goals (Table 6-6). Ordinary expenditure tended to pull ahead of revenue, and there was no surplus with which to finance development expenditures. Taken together, development expenditure and public entity deficits threw the public sector budget into substantial deficit. Approximately 60 per cent of this deficit was absorbed by means of bank financing, and the remainder by external loans (line 8, Table 6-6).

TABLE 6-6 Sudan Central Government Budget, 1969/70 to 1972/73 (£S. m)

	Actual			*Provisional actual*
	1969/70	*1970/71*	*1971/72*	*1972/73*
1. Central government revenue	136.6	160.7	162.3	174.3
2. Central government ordinary expenditure	135.0	157.3	171.9	190.7
3. Current surplus or deficit(−)	1.6	3.4	−9.6	−16.4
4. Development expenditure	28.6	26.6	29.8	29.6
5. Public entities: Net surplus or deficit (−)	−12.4	−15.8	−16.0	0.5
6. Other public sector operations Net surplus or deficit (−)	2.6	5.5	1.3	2.1
7. *Total public sectors deficit*	−37.0	−33.5	−54.1	−43.4
Financing of deficit:				
8. External loans (gross)	14.5	13.3	21.9	20.7
9. Bank Financing (net)	21.5	20.2	32.2	22.7
10. Sales of government securities to private sector	1.0	—	—	—

SOURCE Bank of Sudan, *Fourteenth Annual Report*, March 1974, p. 67.

1 *Ordinary Revenues*

Ordinary revenues of the central government include a variety of taxes, profits from government enterprises, and other revenues. In 1971–2 the Sudan derived a high proportion of revenues from indirect taxes which include taxes on international transactions (39 per cent of revenues), excise and consumption duties (18 per cent of revenues), and the sugar monopoly tax (11 per cent of revenues). These three revenue sources plus the consolidated income tax accounted for 79 per cent of ordinary revenues (Table 6-7). The main revenue sources shifted in importance in the short period FY 1965/66 to FY 1971/72. In FY 1965/66 taxes on international transactions accounted for 44 per cent of total revenues. The decline to 39 per cent in 1971/72 reflects a pattern that follows in most

TABLE 6-7 Sudan Central Government Budget – Ordinary Revenues (£S.m.)

	Actual			*1972/73*	
	1969/70	*1970/71*	*1971/72*	*Provisional actual estimates*	*Budget estimates*
Consolidated income tax	11.8	15.1	17.8	19.6	24.8
Pension contributions	0.9	0.7	2.1	1.1	3.5
Sugar monopoly tax	18.0	18.7	17.0	14.4	10.0
Excise and consumption duties	20.0	26.3	28.4	29.1	30.0
Taxes on international transactions	49.4	59.4	62.6	65.4	63.9
Stamp duty	1.4	1.2	1.3	1.2	2.0
Fees and charges	11.8	14.1	5.9	10.8	12.9
Property receipts	10.8	13.0	4.0	8.1	9.5
Profits received from banking system	2.6	5.4	4.3	5.9	4.0
Public enterprises	—	0.8	1.0	1.4	8.4
Other revenues	4.7	2.4	2.9	5.0	5.1
Reimbursement and inter-dept. sources	7.9	7.6	8.1	8.9	8.9
	136.6	160.7	162.3	174.3	188.7

SOURCE Bank of Sudan, *Fourteenth Annual Report*, March 1974, p. 68.

nations as they move from pre-industrial to a somewhat more industrialised status. A developing country such as the Sudan finds it convenient to employ this form of taxation, which includes export taxes, multiple exchange rates (which tend to penalise exporters of cotton and gum arabic), and government export monopolies. In effect, the export tax on cotton accrues to the Gezira Cotton Marketing Board, which finances the management of the Gezira scheme. According to Levin, there are certain features in the structure of export economies such as the Sudan which lend justification to use of multiple exchange rates or differential taxation of specific export and import commodities. The rationale for a single exchange rate and uniform duties on foreign traded goods is in the expectation that factors of production receiving lower returns will shift to more profitable areas of employment, where they are most efficient.[16] This shift of resources depends on domestic factor mobility, where factors respond to lower income by shifting to higher-paying employment. In many of the export economies this condition of domestic mobility is not present. Restricted mobility in the Sudan prevents this shifting and results in a continued lower return to the immobile producer.

In the period FY 1965/66 to FY 1971/72 income tax revenues increased in relative importance from 6 per cent to 11 per cent of overall revenues. Revenues from income taxes increased significantly in FY 1970/71 as a result of the Income Tax Amendment of 1971. Taxes are levied on three sources of income including business profits, rent on land and buildings, and personal incomes. Income tax rates on corporations begin at 25 per cent and increase progressively to a level of 60 per cent on the highest tranche of profits (over £S.50,000 for public corporations and over £S.20,000 for private family corporations). These rates are reflected in Table 6-8A. Rates on earnings of individual and partnership business profits begin at 15 per cent and progress to 60 per cent (Table 6-8B). Rates on personal incomes begin at 10 per cent and progress to 60 per cent (Table 6-8C). In the case of personal income taxes, and taxes applied to individual partnership business earnings there is an exemption of the first £S.300 from taxes. The 1971 income tax reform has improved on the responsiveness of tax revenues to changes in national income. We return to this concept of income elasticity of tax revenues below.

Excise and consumption duties represent the second largest source of tax revenue in the Sudan. In the period FY 1965/66 to FY 1971/72 this source of revenue increased in importance from 10 per cent to 18 per cent of government revenues. It is unfortunate that such heavy reliance must be placed on regressive taxes of this type. One reason for the dependence on excise and consumption taxes is the difficulty in finding tax bases which are measurable and subject to administrative control and enforcement. Tax administration poses serious problems in less developed countries such as the Sudan. One study has indicated that basic aspects of administrative procedure are extremely difficult or impossible of execution.[17] Administrative procedures that are especially difficult to carry out successfully include locating the taxpayer, obtaining compliance, tax collection, and invoking penalties.

While excise taxation dates back several decades prior to Sudanese independence, the revenue from excises was negligible in view of the embryonic status of industry. After independence local industries grew at an impressive pace and the list of commodities covered by excise taxes is lengthy. In addition to extended coverage the rates of excise and consumption taxes have been increased several times. It is not surprising therefore that excise and consumption taxes have demonstrated a rising share of total tax receipts. The low price elasticity and high income elasticity of demand for liquor, tobacco and other taxed products have assured rising revenues given upward revision of tax rates. Wide use of excise and sales taxes is logical if the revenue lost from import substitution is to be offset.

TABLE 6-8A Business Income Tax Schedule – Corporations

Private-family		*Public-owned joint stock Co.*	
Income tranche (£S.)	*Applicable rate of tax (%)*	*Income tranche (£S.)*	*Applicable rate of tax (%)*
First 1,000	25	First 1,000	25
Next 9,000	40	Next 9,000	40
Next 10,000	50	Next 10,000	45
Additional income	60	Next 30,000	50
		Additional income	60

TABLE 6-8B Business Income Tax Schedule – Individual and Partnership

Income tranche	*Applicable rate of tax*
First 200	Exempt*
Next 200	15
Next 500	20
Next 3,000	30
Next 6,000	40
Next 20,000	50
Additional income	60

TABLE 6-8C Personal Income Tax Schedule

Income tranche (£S.)	*Applicable rate of tax (%)*
First 300	Exempt*
Next 400	10
Next 1,000	15
Next 1,000	20
Next 2,000	30
Next 2,000	40
Next 3,000	50
Additional income	60

* In the case of bachelor individuals, the first £S.200 is exempt and the next £S.100 is taxed at 1 per cent under personal income taxes, and at 5 per cent under business income taxes. Non-resident corporations are taxed in the same way as private-family corporations.

SOURCE Department of Taxation, Democratic Republic of the Sudan.

Moreover, local industries in the Sudan owe their existence to government help in the form of tax relief and protection against foreign imported goods.[18]

A fundamental problem of taxation in the Sudan is the low income elasticity of tax revenues given an increase in national income. This elasticity concept may be defined as the percentage change in tax yields associated with a given percentage change in national income. Nimeiri has found a low elasticity of total revenues and tax revenues given changes in gross domestic product in the Sudan (Table 6-9). The low elasticity of indirect taxation contrasts sharply with the high elasticity of direct taxation (a product of the steeply progressive rates on direct taxes introduced late in the period studied by Nimeiri). Indirect taxes account for a high proportion of total tax revenues (78 per cent) and therefore 'impart inelasticity to the system as a whole'. The low elasticity of indirect taxes is explained by Nimeiri as due to the extremely low elasticity of import duties, export duties, and royalties.[19] He refers to a study by Thorn which compared the elasticity of expenditure and revenues of the Sudan and fourteen African–Asian countries. Thorn's study indicated that the Sudan has one of the lowest tax revenue elasticities of all countries, and unusually high expenditure elasticity relative to tax revenue elasticity.[20]

TABLE 6-9 Elasticity of Government Tax Revenues and Expenditures in the Sudan, 1959–69

Variable	*Elasticity value*	*% of total revenue*	*% of tax revenue*
Government current revenue	1.5	—	—
Total revenue	0.7	—	—
Tax revenue	0.9	—	—
Non-tax revenue	0.3	42	—
Direct taxes	3.1	13	22
Indirect taxes	0.77	45	78

SOURCE Sayed M. Nimeiri, 'Income Elasticity of Tax Structure in the Sudan', *Sudan Journal of Economic and Social Studies* (Khartoum University Press), summer 1974, p. 41.

Implications from the analysis of income elasticity are important. First, the analysis suggests that the tax structure (in 1959–69) was inadequate due to its inflexibility and low income elasticity. An important requirement for effective budgetary management is a rate of growth of government revenues that approximates growth in expenditures. In the Sudan failure to generate additional revenues or control the upward trend of government expenditure would lead to a widening gap between revenues and expenditures, and inflation. Second, an ineffective tax system in the face of growing public expenditure forces the government to participate in ownership and operation of productive enterprises and other ventures that yield revenues. While there may be nothing inherently wrong with this approach, there can be harmful side-effects such as unfair competition of publicly owned versus privately owned industry.

Numerous suggestions have been made for tax reform in the direction of enhancing the income elasticity of taxes. The following summarises approaches that might prove to be more feasible:[21]

(1) Shift the emphasis of indirect taxation from taxes on foreign trade to taxes based on domestic trade and production.
(2) Domestic excise taxes have a higher income elasticity than taxes on foreign trade, and should gradually replace the latter.
(3) Improvement and rationalisation of income taxes could be effected by reduction of exemption limits, increase of tax rates, elimination of under-assessment of business profits, and improved collection of the rent tax.
(4) Introduction of new direct taxes that grow faster than GDP such as the wealth tax, capital gains taxes, and gift-inheritance taxes.
(5) Tax administrative machinery in the Sudan should be given more attention. Outmoded tax laws and traditional taxes such as the Hut Tax and Animal Tax should be discarded.

2 *Expenditures*

The central government budget distinguishes between Ordinary and Development Expenditures. In the period 1970–2 Development Expenditures represented 15 per cent of total spending by the central government (Table 6-10). Ordinary Expenditures, which constitute the remaining 85 per cent of government spending, are dominated by defence, local government, debt service, and educational expenses. Defence spending accounts for over one-fourth of Ordinary Expenditures, exceeds Development Expenditures by a wide margin, and has been the largest single expenditure component in the budget since 1961. Defence expenditures grew at a rapid pace in the period 1965–71 in connection with internal insurrection, general concern in the Middle East with the Arab–Israeli War and tensions which followed fear of a Communist plot, and the need to establish internal order under the Presidency of General Nimeiri. It is unfortunate that so large a part of the budget of the Sudan must be devoted to defence. However, internal and Middle East pressures have manifested themselves repeatedly.

TABLE 6-10 Sudan Central Government Budget – Ordinary Expenditures and Development Expenditures (£S. m.)

ORDINARY EXPENDITURES

	Actual			1972–3	
	1969/70	1970/71	1971/72	Provisional actual	Budget estimates
Defence and security	40.5	46.8	47.4	50.3	50.2
Education	13.3	13.9	14.7	18.0	17.9
Health	7.6	7.9	8.5	9.6	9.6
Other social services	3.9	3.6	5.0	5.9	6.5
Ministry of Agriculture, Food and National Resources	9.8	9.4	11.0	14.0	14.8
Ministry of communications and Transport	6.4	6.9	6.8	8.8	9.3
Other economic services	3.8	3.2	3.1	3.8	4.3
Local government	20.1	17.6	27.8	25.0	15.9
Debt servicing	8.9	9.9	15.6	10.1	15.9
Other	20.7	38.1	32.0	39.2	42.6
TOTAL	135.0	157.3	171.9	190.7	187.0

DEVELOPMENT EXPENDITURES

	1970/71	1971/72	1972/73	
	Actual	Actual	Actual	Approved allocations
Agriculture and irrigation	9.7	10.4	11.1	24.2
Industry and mining	1.6	1.5	1.9	7.3
Transport and communications	3.1	3.0	6.6	13.0
C.E.W.C.	3.6	3.4	2.5	4.3
Local government	2.8	1.4	1.0	2.0
Social services	3.0	3.8	3.5	5.6
Other including special allocations for Southern Region	2.9	6.3	3.0	9.1
TOTAL	26.7	29.8	29.6	65.5

SOURCE Bank of Sudan, *Fourteenth Annual Report*, March 1974, pp. 69–70.

Development Expenditures play a strategic role in the Sudan. We have noted that public sector development spending accounted for 52 per cent and 54 per cent of total development spending in each of the five-year periods 1965–70 and 1970–5, respectively. Also, government development expenditures focus on agriculture-irrigation and certain infrastructure sectors (railways, electric power, and communications) that enjoy a government monopoly position.

In short, given the critical need for additional capacity in infrastructure to accommodate general economic advance, and the heavy dependence of employment, income and foreign exchange earnings on agricultural production, government development spending assumes an essential character.

3 *Borrowing*

The overall budget depicted in Table 6-6 reflects annual public sector deficits of between £S.33 million and £S.54 million over the period 1969–73. Approximately 60 per cent of this was financed by bank financing and the remainder by external loans. Sudan external borrowing is discussed in Chapter 7, which deals with external economic relations. Our purpose in this section is to discuss the means used and controls exercised over bank financing of budgetary deficits.

Excessive reliance on bank financing of central government budgetary deficits presents serious risks in the direction of generating inflation, exerting negative resource allocation effects, and impairing the nation's credit standing in the eyes of international lenders. It is for these reasons that the Sudan has imposed limitations on the use of commercial bank and central bank credit by the central government.

The Treasury Bill Act of 1966 as subsequently amended permits the government to borrow by means of Treasury bill issue provided that the total value of bills outstanding at any time does not exceed £S.10 million. In 1971 this act was amended to increase the ceiling to £S.15 million, and a further amendment in 1973 raised the ceiling to £S.25 million. By year-end 1973 commercial bank holdings of Treasury bills was £S.18.25 million.[22]

According to Section 57 of the Bank of Sudan Act as amended in 1971, central bank loans to the government are limited to 10 per cent of the current estimate of the government revenue during the financial year in which the loans are advanced.[23] These loans are repayable within six months after the end of the fiscal year and are designated 'Temporary Advances to the Government' on the balance sheet of the Bank of Sudan. The central government has additional flexibility in adjusting its liquidity position by means of further drawing on its deposits with the central bank and commercial banks. At year-end 1973 these deposits were £S.4.8 million and £S.2.2 million, respectively.

Originally advances under Section 57 of the Bank of Sudan Act to the government and its boards and agencies were not permitted to exceed 15 per cent of total ordinary revenue. The Act was amended so that advances to government boards are to be provided under Section 57A and are not deductible from the central government ceiling under Section 57. The volume of these loans outstanding at December 1973 was £S.48.9 million.

At times the central government has issued long-term debt in the form of 5 per cent stock. At year-end 1973 a total of £S.494 thousand of 5 per cent 1977 stock was held by various financial institutions, companies, and private investors.

It should be noted in closing that the opportunity for marketing and distributing central government debt securities is very limited. The most logical investors are the commercial banks and the central bank. However, it is desirable to have a broader market for government securities so that when deficit financing is necessary it can be achieved by sale to the non-bank public and with a minimum of inflationary pressures.

F EMERGENCE OF FINANCE CAPITALISM

Economic growth requires increased investment, and a more effective mobilisation of savings flows so that the most productive investment opportunities receive financing. Effective mobilisation of savings in a national economy requires that savers be able to exchange their savings for a type of asset that conforms to their overall portfolio requirements. Choices available to savers ordinarily could include any of six basic asset categories: namely (1) non-productive physical assets (gold, silver, jewellery), (2) productive physical assets (cattle, farms, producer's equipment), (3) money and near-money assets (currency, demand and time deposits), (4) shares of limited liability companies, (5) debt instruments of government units or business firms, and (6) liabilities of non-bank financial intermediaries. Earlier we have seen that category (3) has grown in importance in the Sudan and that the ratio of M_2 to GDP increased in the period 1956–72 from 0.102 to 0.224. Also, we have observed that the expansion of liquidity in the Sudan financial system has been impressive, with the non-bank public increasing its share of liquidity to 67.7 per cent of total liquidity in the Sudan in 1974.

Gold hoarding and the holding of jewellery and other non-productive assets is another factor to be taken into account when assessing the capacity of the Sudan to mobilise savings. Personal savings in the Sudan are typically hoarded in land, cattle, and gold jewellery. The amounts of gold hoarded in the Sudan are unknown, but United Nations estimates place gold hoards in adjacent Middle East countries at close to 20 per cent of national income.[24] It can be argued that gold hoards could be mobilised for productive saving-investment in the Sudan by creation of safe and profitable investment opportunities and suitable alternative financial assets.[25]

Alternatives to gold hoarding include shares of limited liability companies, debt instruments, and liabilities of non-bank financial intermediaries. Aside from the commercial banks the Post Office Savings Bank is the only institution in the country that accepts savings type deposits. Depositors in the Post Office Savings Bank include individuals, business firms, insurance companies, pension and provident funds and government agencies. The Post Office savings facility is available in every branch of the Post Office, extending its coverage to rural areas where there are no commercial bank branches.

Another potentially important source of capital funds is the insurance companies and pension funds. The volume of their investments in bank deposit accounts and government securities indicates that these institutions could contribute materially to capital formation in the Sudan. Finally, we should note that a form of 'mutual fund' operates in the Sudan as informal associations operated mainly by housewives. These *sandug* or 'funds' accumulate small individual savings to meet personal needs such as marriage and birth expenses, purchase of consumer durables, or travel expenses. Their expansion indicates a growing habit of savings among the Sudanese people, which by careful effort might be channelled in part into financing economic development.

1 *Share Issue and Stock Exchange Facility*

Development of share issue and ownership can further the evolution in the Sudan toward more effective mobilisation of saving for capital investment. At present individual and family-owned enterprises represent the most important form of ownership of business in the Sudan. Most public companies are held by closely knit groups. Writing in 1970 Saeed noted that the shares of only five Sudanese companies were distributed widely enough to be transacted, namely Sudan Commercial Bank, Sudan Cinema Company, Nile Cement Company, National Cigarettes Company, and Khartoum Spinning and Weaving Company (the Sudan Commercial Bank was nationalised shortly after Saeed prepared his study for publication).[26] In the period 1961–8 the number of shares of these five companies issued and outstanding averaged 1443.7 thousand, and the average value of shares issued each year was £S.2701.8 thousand. The average value of shares transacted each year was only £S.127.6 thousand, or 4.65 per cent of those outstanding. Clearly, the market for shares was very narrow. One measure that could be utilised to widen ownership and marketability would be to keep the issue price of company shares low.

In 1967 the Council of Ministers decided that all import trade should be Sudanised, and that public companies whose shares were available to the public be granted import concessions for all essential commodities (coffee, tea, pharmaceutical goods, flour). To avoid monopolistic tendencies it was required that more than one public company be established for each imported commodity and that individual holdings of shares should not exceed a predetermined maximum number. This decision was not implemented, but in 1969 the Companies Ordinance Act provided for promotion of private investment by the incorporation of concession companies open to participation by the public. The government took immediate action by declaring that imports of coffee, tea, and salt were to be transferred to the private sector. Up to this time imports of these products had been a government monopoly. Public companies with shares issued to importers hold the import concession. In September 1969 the Sudan Tea Company was established, and in the field of exports the Gum Arabic Company was established.

In the absence of a stock exchange in the Sudan public and private debt and equity instruments are traded on an *ad hoc* basis. The central bank has maintained a record of potential buyers and sellers for Sudan Government Bonds, with the objective of matching bids and offers. Moreover, commercial banks have agreed to assist buyers and sellers in effecting trades. Insofar as equities are concerned a buyer or seller would have to run an advertisement in the newspapers. It has been reported that several commission agencies and brokers initiated dealing in stocks, but low volume would make it difficult to extract sufficient profit from this activity.

A strong argument can be developed for organisation of a stock exchange in Khartoum. Advantages would include availability of a centralised market facility, enhanced liquidity and valuation of shares, and encouragement of formation of limited liability companies as a means of business organisation in the Sudan. The stock exchange could meet once or twice a week until volume of share trading reached a level warranting a full weekly schedule. Legal safeguards can be provided concerning rules for flotation of securities, operation and reporting by public companies, operation of the stock exchange and rules for trading, and nature of government supervision. Organisation of a stock exchange would assist in the evolution of the Sudanese financial structure toward finance capitalism.

7 External Economic Relations

Successful growth and prosperity of the Sudanese economy depends on favourable external economic and financial relationships. The Sudan is a relatively open economy. In the period 1968–72 exports represented over 18 per cent of GNP. A shortage of domestic savings and investment capital requires an infusion of foreign capital funds. Lack of technology and organisational expertise makes it necessary for the country to avail itself of imported technicians and business specialists, again placing pressure on the limited resources that are available to cover import requirements.

Government policy continues to be a prime moving force where development and improvement of favourable trading and financing relationships are concerned. The government has proven itself to be flexible and able to adopt new priorities given changes in world economic conditions and opportunities. For example, during the 1970s self-sufficiency in basic food staples has become a higher priority item than commodity exports. Consequently, wheat planting has supplanted cotton culture in those irrigated areas considered suitable to this substitution. Underlying this policy shift is a projected static world cotton market and escalating grain feed prices in the international commodity markets.[1]

A Foreign Exchange and Balance of Payments

Since 1957 the Sudan has been a separate and independent monetary area. Until that date the Egyptian pound was the official currency, with a par value of $2.8716 which had been established in September 1949 when the United Kingdom and sterling area trading partners devalued their currencies *vis-à-vis* the US dollar. The Sudan currency continues to retain this same parity relationship with the US dollar. The Sudan foreign exchange system is managed by the Bank of Sudan, which quotes official rates for transactions in US dollars and other currencies. A rate of £S.1 = US$2.50 is applied to all exchange transactions other than the proceeds from exports of cotton and gum arabic, to which the rate of £S.1 = US$2.8716 applies. The less favourable exchange rate on Sudanese pounds received by exporters of cotton and gum arabic reflects an effective exchange tax of 15 per cent.

The Bank of Sudan operates a relatively thorough exchange control system. Imports and other foreign payments are approved within the framework of an annual foreign exchange budget drawn up by the Ministry of National Economy and approved by the Economic Council.[2] Transactions with countries with which the Sudan has concluded bilateral payments agreements (including Egypt, the German Democratic Republic, India and Poland) are settled through the relevant bilateral account in Sudanese pounds or pounds sterling. For imports that require individual licensing, licenses may be obtained from the Ministry of Finance and National Economy, and validated by the central bank's exchange control department. Ordinarily, private sector imports (with the exception of capital goods, heavy trucks, and medicines which are exempt) require an advance deposit of 2 per cent. An exemption is provided when suppliers' credits are available with a minimum of two years' maturity.

All exports require a licence, with the exception of cotton and gum arabic. Authorised banks may approve export requests except in cases where credit is provided, in which case approval is required from the Bank of Sudan. The proceeds of exports must be repatriated and surrendered through an authorised bank. Occasionally, exports of some commodities may be temporarily suspended due to supply conditions (some meat exports in 1974–5). Moreover, export duties may be adjusted upward or downward based upon supply conditions for the commodities affected.

The Development and Promotion of Industrial Investment Acts provide for the registration of inward foreign capital for investment in industry. When registered such capital may receive a guarantee of repatriation of original capital, and remittance of profits.

The exchange control system in the Sudan is designed to accomplish several government policy objectives. First, it permits the central bank to maintain a minimal amount of hard currency reserves relative to merchandise imports (reserves of the Sudan are equivalent to approximately two months of imports). Second, central government priorities can be more effectively enforced. Finally, a viable balance of payments is maintained, while at the same time the government is completely free to pursue macroeconomic and price-wage policies it considers appropriate in light of emerging conditions and circumstances.

The balance of payments reflects a near equality between merchandise exports and imports. The export side is dominated by cotton, which in the period 1968–73 accounted for over 55 per cent of the value of merchandise exports.[3] In the same time period direct purchases by the government accounted for close to 30 per cent of merchandise imports.

Service transactions tend to generate a net deficit in the Sudanese balance of payments. The extent of these deficits has been circumscribed by government policy in the case of travel payments and payments to emigrants. During the 1960s invisible exports represented over 14 per cent of merchandise in exports while invisible imports fluctuated at close to 25 per cent of merchandise imports. Efforts of the Sudanese government to reduce the importance of invisible imports in the balance of payments included reduction in the foreign exchange allowance for travel (1959 and 1966), establishment of the Sudan Shipping Line (a joint venture between the Sudan government and Yugoslavia) in 1961, and development of the national airline (Sudan Airways). Structural shifts in the direction of Sudan's exports have dampened the growth of shipping expenses, e.g., displacement of the United Kingdom as major buyer of Sudanese cotton, and of India and EEC countries as buyers of other primary products.[4] The closing of the Suez Canal in 1967 resulted in a 50 per cent increase in freight charges that had to be borne by the Sudan economy. A similar closing in 1973 again inflated transportation charges. In this case the Canal remained closed until 1975, again resulting in substantially increased transportation costs on imports and exports.

The capital account in the balance of payments reflects an impressively large number of official loans and investments by foreign governments and specialist institutions. These loans and investments have been derived from a wide range of sources including the World Bank and related agencies, Western European governments, Eastern European countries, Mainland China, Middle Eastern countries, and agencies of the United Nations, suggesting that the Sudanese government has been successful in maintaining favourable economic relationships with nations of all political leanings. In the period 1968–71 repayments on official loans grew more rapidly than drawings on such credits, and in 1971 exceeded drawings by £S.3.3 million. With the achievement of more settled internal conditions and the termination of hostilities in the Southern Provinces, official loans doubled in value and in number of individual loan agreements. Thus in 1972–3 drawings on official loans increased to over £S.22–25 million (Table 7-1). In recent years net suppliers' credits and short-term capital flows have been small in amount.

In the period 1968–73 the Sudan enjoyed balance of payments surpluses in two years (1969 and 1973) and deficits in the remaining four years. Due to the active role of the government in external

TABLE 7-1 Official Loans to the Sudan (£S. m.)

	Drawings	*Repayments*	*Net flow*
1968	9.6	3.5	6.1
1969	17.8	4.5	13.3
1970	8.1	7.6	0.5
1971	8.0	11.3	−3.3
1972	22.3	12.2	10.1
1973	25.2	17.1	8.1

SOURCE Bank of Sudan, *Fourteenth Annual Report*, 1973, pp. 82–3.

economic affairs, which includes fairly detailed exchange controls, supervision of the flow of foreign trade, negotiation of and administration of bilateral payments agreements, and securing of foreign loans, it is not overly difficult for government policy-makers to close a balance of payments deficit. The costs incurred in regaining better balance in external payments may take various forms including reduced imports for consumption, higher prices of imported goods, increased internal taxation to absorb expenditures, deferral in completion of certain capital investment projects, or other costs. Given the wide range of possible measures available to government policy-makers in the Sudan, it is probable that no single measure will be focused on, but that a number of policy measures will be applied to the economy at any given time.

B FLOW AND PATTERN OF EXTERNAL TRADE

Foreign trade assumes a vital role in the Sudan. This is particularly the case in connection with the need to generate foreign exchange earnings and the financing of capital equipment imports.[5] Like many other African nations, the Sudan derives a substantial share of its merchandise export earnings from only a few commodity categories. Cotton represents by far the largest single export commodity, accounting for over half of exports. In the period 1966–9 gum arabic was the second most important export, accounting for over 10 per cent of merchandise exports. The value of exports of gum arabic declined in the period 1969–73, and by 1973 gum arabic had fallen to become the fifth most important export commodity. In that year groundnuts, sesame, and oilcake and meal ranked second, third, and fourth respectively as export earners.

Sudan's exports are dominated by products of agriculture, and cattle and meat products (live animals, meat, and hides and skins). A small but growing export trade in minerals and extractive products (chrome ore, iron, and manganese) offers promise of expanded opportunities for foreign exchange earnings. Exports of manufactures is in an embryonic stage of development at this time.

Sudan's exports are characterised by extreme fluctuations. Export growth tends to be followed by relative decline or stagnation. Changes in imports have lagged behind changes in exports, so that the trade balance has oscillated between surplus and deficit.[6] These fluctuations have made it difficult for the government to follow a consistent fiscal policy.

The Sudan's imports are far more diversified than its exports. In 1973 the principal categories were transport equipment (16.7 per cent), machinery and spare parts (13.2 per cent), chemicals and pharmaceuticals (12.5 per cent), textiles (10.7 per cent), and sugar (9.7 per cent).[7] In a supply-hungry economy such as the Sudan, it is not surprising to find spare parts for machinery and transport equipment accounting for a large share of the value of imports (17 per cent). However, it is surprising to see that textiles continue to account for a major share of the value of imports in light of the availability of domestic cotton and the advantages possible from extending textile manufacturing in the direction of greater domestic value added.

Due to the lack of domestic substitutes the Sudan's demand for imports has been relatively inelastic.[8] In 1973 foodstuffs represented over 22 per cent of the value of imports entering the Sudan. Sugar, wheat, tea and coffee represented the greater part of this total. It should be noted that current economic and industrial development plans call for self-sufficiency in sugar. Moreover, the government has initiated plans to shift some irrigated areas from cotton to wheat production. In light of the weak world market situation for cotton and the projected shortages of food including grain foods, this shift in agriculture should be helpful to the balance of trade of the Sudan.

The directional pattern of Sudan's merchandise trade has been subject to significant changes during the early 1970s. On the export side, the USSR, which had been the largest customer of the Sudan in 1970 (purchasing 16 per cent of the Sudan's exports) became an inconsiderable buyer. Far Eastern countries (China and Japan) advanced in relative importance. Finally, Saudi Arabia and France moved into the top ten category as customers of the Sudan. On the import side the shifts in importance were equally significant. While the UK retained its long-standing role as principal supplier to the Sudan, other countries (US, Brazil, China, West Germany and Japan) increased in relative importance as exporters to the Sudan. The USSR and India declined in importance, with India experiencing an absolute reduction in sales to the Sudan.

Political and economic factors both play an important role in determining a country's trading ties with other nations. In the case

TABLE 7-2 Direction of Trade of the Sudan

Major customers for Sudan's exports	*1970*	*1973*	*Major suppliers of Sudan's imports*	*1970*	*1973*
	(£S.'000)				
China	6,180	22,746	UK	20,118	27,366
Japan	9,322	16,887	US	3,067	11,568
Italy	10,744	16,866	India	13,288	11,331
W. Germany	10,582	13,874	Brazil	3	11,317
France	2,350	9,247	China	4,252	10,233
India	10,270	8.878	W. Germany	7,851	9,934
Netherlands	3,619	7,313	Japan	5,923	9,098
Egypt	5,644	5,767	USSR	8,569	9,057
UK	6,177	5,453	France	2,181	6,358
Saudi Arabia	2,185	4,370	Italy	2,043	5,315
Total exports	103,914	152,172	Total imports	100,120	151,841

SOURCE Bank of Sudan, *Fourteenth Annual Report*, 1973, p. 92.

of the Sudan a major shift in political relations with the USSR explains the rapid decline in trade that took place in 1970–3. On the other hand improved political and economic ties with China have resulted in the provision of substantial credits by China to finance development and construction projects (including a major conference center in Khartoum), and in the conclusion of bilateral trade agreements between the two countries. US government policy has become more amenable to extended trade and credit relationships with the Sudan, permitting a rise in exports to the Sudan. Finally, proximity to oil-rich Saudi Arabia has resulted in the expansion of food and other exports to that country. In turn Saudi Arabia has become more interested in investing in the Sudan to develop the potential of this country as an important neighbouring supplier of commodities necessary to the economic development of the Saudi Arabian peninsula.

During the early 1970s the Sudan has conducted its external trade with six countries on the basis of pre-negotiated bilateral payments agreements. These agreements provide for the type of merchandise to be purchased by each trading partner from the other, the total amount of trade to take place in each direction valued in a specific currency, provisions for swing credits or overdrafts, and methods for utilising accumulated balances in settling future trade between the partner countries. Several advantages can be derived by a country from the use of bilateral agreements. A producer of a staple commodity (such as cotton) can sell that commodity off the competitive world market. This could prove to be an advantage when the trend in world market prices is downward. Second, availability and use of swing credit facilities can increase the total volume of trade between the two trading partners. Third, bilateral payments agreements represent a discrete form of trade preferences. Fourth, such agreements permit trading partners to maintain a domestic price structure that is not totally related to the world trade price structure. Finally, bilateral payments agreements provide a convenient means of negotiating an expansion of trade and credits.

In 1973 the flow of merchandise trade of the Sudan in connection with use of bilateral agreements represented 9.3 per cent of export trade and 10.9 per cent of import trade (Table 7-3). Characteristically, trade with the six bilateral countries tends to be concentrated

TABLE 7-3 Flow of Trade with Bilateral Payments Agreement Countries (£S.'000)

Bilateral partner	*1973* *Exports*	*Imports*
Czechoslovakia	1,209	1,679
East Germany	756	675
Hungary	696	1,113
Poland	696	1,218
Egypt	7,904	3,287
India	2,830	8,675
Total	14,091	16,647
As % of Sudan's Total	9.3%	10.9%

SOURCE Bank of Sudan, *Fourteenth Annual Report* (1973), pp. 41–7.

into only a few major commodities. For example, in trade with the four Eastern European countries cotton exports account for over 65 per cent of the total. In trade with Egypt textiles represent over two-thirds of Sudan's imports from Egypt. On the export side 90 per cent of Sudan's sales to Egypt fall under four categories, including camels (31 per cent), cattle and meat (22 per cent), sesame (15 per cent) and cotton seed oil (22 per cent). Trade with India is heavily concentrated on the export side with 90 per cent of exports in cotton and 10 per cent in gum arabic. Three commodity categories dominate the Sudan's imports from India, namely tea (44 per cent), jute (22 per cent), and textiles (13 per cent).

The Sudan faces serious future difficulties in its bilateral agreements. The heavy concentration of cotton exports in the face of a weak world demand situation suggests more difficult negotiating terms. The desire of the Sudan to expand textiles manufacturing at home also reduces the opportunities to trade for lower cost imports. Textiles account for a major share of imports from India and Egypt. Finally, residual credit balances (at year-end 1973 the Sudan was indebted to India, but a creditor of Egypt) present a problem since these balances are not easily transferable, and must be worked out via extensions of payments agreements in future years, or negotiated in terms of purchasing commodities or services not listed in the original payments agreement.

C FLOW OF INVESTMENT

In the case of less developed countries the availability of foreign investment capital may be considered one of four major constraints on domestic capital formation. The other three constraints are domestic savings, capital absorptive capacity, and foreign exchange receipts.[9] Based on data contained in Table 7-4 it can be observed that in the period 1965–72 new foreign loans and grants represented close to one-fourth of gross fixed domestic investment.[10] In the same period gross fixed investment was slightly in excess of 12 per cent of GDP.

The saving which financed fixed capital formation came for the most part from domestic sources (domestic saving was equivalent to 9 per cent of GDP). Nevertheless, from the data contained in Table 7-4, approximately one-fourth of this saving originated in other countries and was made available in the form of foreign loans and grants. A domestic saving rate of less than 10 per cent of GNP makes it very difficult for a country to achieve self-sustaining growth without significant doses of external loans and assistance. Assuming a capital-output ratio of 3 and a domestic savings/investment ratio

TABLE 7-4 Foreign Loans and Grants to the Sudan Relative to Gross Domestic Fixed Capital Formation

	Loans 1	*Grants* 2	*Total* 3	*Gross domestic invest-ment US$ m,* 4	*% of GDP* 5	*Loans and grants as % of invest-ment* 6	*Loans as % of invest-ment* 7
1965–8	45.0	8.6	53.6	190.96	12.6	28.1	23.5
1969–72	39.0	17.7	56.7	203.55	12.1	27.9	19.2

SOURCES World Bank, *Annual Report*, 1974, pp. 96–7; Democratic Republic of the Sudan, *Statistical Yearbook*, 1973, Table XIV–1.

of 10 per cent, the maximum growth rate of GNP will be 3.33 per cent per annum. A population growth rate of 2.8–3.1 per cent (the rate of population growth in the Sudan in 1960–70) brings the growth in *per capita* GNP to only 0.5 per cent per annum or less. This is not sufficient to achieve any significant economic advance.

In the period 1965–72 the debt service payments of the Sudan on its external public debt increased steadily as a percentage of exports of goods and services, rising from 5.5 per cent in 1965, to 6.8 per cent in 1968, to 9.1 per cent in 1970, and to 12.3 per cent in 1972.[11] In short, the debt service ratio more than doubled, reflecting a relatively moderate growth in export earnings (approximately 9–10 per cent per annum), and a rapid surge in debt service payments for interest and amortisation of principle. During this period Sudan's foreign trade was kept closely in balance. From this it would appear that growth in the capacity to export (influencing the foreign exchange gap) operates as a significant constraint on the growth process in the Sudan in at least two ways. First, the debt service ratio has risen rapidly due to the differential in growth of export earnings and required debt service, placing pressure on the country's future capacity to borrow. Second, a more rapid growth of exports would directly provide the foreign exchange required to pay for additional imports of capital goods.

The foreign exchange gap is not the only significant constraint on growth. Two other constraints have been operative in the Sudan, including the limited capital absorptive capacity of the domestic economy, and the relatively low level of domestic savings.

The diversity of sources of foreign capital is most interesting. These have included Kuwaiti loans for the Sudan Railway and for manufacturing enterprises; inter-governmental loans from a number of Western European countries (W. Germany, France and Sweden); a loan from China for construction of a conference centre in Khartoum; FAO aid; loans from private banks (Swiss); a British loan to develop water pump irrigation facilities; several loans from Saudi Arabia to develop food production; US government credits in connection with commodity sales; several Egyptian loans; and a number of World Bank credits. The scope of World Bank lending to the Sudan has expanded in the decade of the 1970s, partly due to the higher priority given by that international organisation to the least developed countries, in part due to higher priorities for food and agricultural projects, and in part due to the settlement of the Southern problem and subsiding of hostilities in the Southern provinces of the Sudan.

In fiscal year 1974 the World Bank extended three loans to the Sudan, one for agricultural development, one for $4 million to expand the Industrial Bank of Sudan's foreign exchange resources to be used in financing private and public sector industrial development projects, and one for development of transport facilities. The latter credit is in the form of an IDA loan for $24 million that will be used to improve the railroads, expand Port Sudan's harbour facilities, and cover the cost of consultant services for airport development studies. The agricultural credit is for $10.7 million and will be used to rehabilitate the Southern region's agriculture, particularly livestock development, cotton and coffee production.

In the fiscal year 1975 the World Bank extended three loans to the Sudan, providing a total of $53 million. The largest loan will be used to provide additional electric generating capacity and transmission facilities. A $20 million IDA credit provides additional funds for completion of the Rahad Irrigation Project. A $10 million loan will be used to improve the educational system in the Sudan, including teacher education, training for out-of-school youths, and a review and analysis of the educational sector.[12]

Of particular concern to the World Bank Group and other leaders is the amount of external debt and the debt servicing relative to capacity to meet debt repayments (measured as a percentage of export earnings). Examining Table 7-5, we can see that in the three-year period 1969–72 there was an increase in total (including undisbursed) debt outstanding of $77.0 million, $61.8 million of which was provided by bilateral official sources. Private banks also were important net suppliers of funds in this period ($21.1 million increase). Multilateral assistance actually declined in this period as repayments exceeded new loans. As noted above the World Bank Group provided IDA credits of $38.7 million in 1974, and $53 million in 1975, with relatively soft repayment terms. While this will increase the amount of external debt outstanding, it will not affect the debt service ratio in the near future due to the terms on which such credits are provided.

TABLE 7-5 External Public Debt Outstanding of the Sudan by Type of Creditor, 1969–73 (US$ m.)

		Including undisbursed					
	Disbursed only	*Total*	*Bilateral official*	*Multi-lateral*	*Suppliers*	*Banks*	*Other*
31.12.69	264.4	305.1	128.9	135.3	15.2	23.6	2.1
31.12.72	297.6	382.1	190.7	137.6	9.1	44.7	0.2
31.12.73	334.6	550.1	275.3	177.9	12.2	84.7	—
Change 1969–72	+33.2	+77.0	+61.8	+2.3	−6.1	+21.1	−1.9
Change 1972–3	+37.0	+168.0	+84.6	+40.3	+3.1	+40.0	−0.2

SOURCE World Bank and IDA, *Annual Reports*; 1971, p. 64; 1974, p. 85; and 1975, p.92.

D GOVERNMENT POLICY AND EXTERNAL RELATIONS

In this section we focus principally on policy aspects of foreign trade and investment. Foreign trade policies are viewed in connection with tariff duties, import substitution and self-sufficiency policies. Foreign investment policies are viewed in connection with measures designed to attract foreign capital, including revision of the investment incentive laws.

Import substitution policies must be considered as they relate to measures designed to promote industrial development. In this connection public investment in factory establishments and allocation of capital funds by the banking sector play important roles in facilitating the attainment of import substitution and greater self-sufficiency along certain product lines. In general import substitution objectives appear to be important in the food processing (flour, sugar, and soap) and clothing-textiles lines of production.

On the export side tariff duties generally are levied for the purpose of generating revenues. Rates cluster in the 2–15 per cent range. Cotton export duties range from 10 per cent on long-staple to 5 per cent on short-staple cotton. Export duties on gum arabic are 5 per cent, plus royalties collected on behalf of local governments.

On the import side commodities fall into three categories insofar as tariff duties are concerned. Due to their overall economic importance, some goods are admitted free of duty, e.g. agricultural equipment. A second category includes consumer goods, which bear relatively high duties (a range of 70 per cent to 200 per cent). High duties on confectionery goods and cigarettes are designed to protect local producers. Low duties (70 per cent) on ready-made clothing and food provisions give recognition to the more necessitous nature of these commodities. Relatively high duties on television sets (100 per cent) and refrigerators (120 per cent) are designed to yield revenue for the government.

A third category consists of capital goods, where tariff rates are kept moderate (20 per cent to 40 per cent). Concessions can be made on these tariff duties by the Minister of Industry. The majority of capital goods imported into the Sudan are given concessions, some relative to the government's programme of investment incentives.

Tariff rates are changed infrequently, usually at the initiative of the Customs Department, Minister of Treasury, or other government department where a specific problem arises in the administration of duties in a particular commodity area. A proposed Unified Customs Ordinance would extend tariff preferences to eight Arab nations including the Sudan. This Ordinance would cover all commodities traded between these Arab countries.

Since 1971 the foreign investment policy of the Sudan has become increasingly more positive in attempting to attract foreign investment. Several factors help explain the increased emphasis given to this objective:

(1) Failure to achieve key economic development plan objectives and resulting slow growth in specific sectors of industry.
(2) Recognition that successful economic growth cannot be sustained without additional inflows of foreign private as well as public investment capital.
(3) Emergence of neighbouring Arab countries (1973–4) as major foreign exchange earners through oil exports.[13]
(4) Desire to offset economic losses incurred as a result of temporary nationalization and confiscation measures taken in 1970.

The government's renewed emphasis on promoting private investment, especially foreign investment, is evidenced by three specific laws passed in the period 1972–4.

(1) The Development and Promotion of Industrial Investment Act, 1972.
(2) The Organisation and Encouragement of Investment in Economic Services Act, 1973.
(3) The Development and Encouragement of Industrial Investment Act, 1974.

Shortly after independence in 1956 the Approved Enterprises Act was passed. This law was designed to encourage certain enterprises to invest in the Sudan. It provided very few concessions, and was replaced in 1967 by the Organisation and Promotion of Industrial Investment Act. This act provided a greater number of concessions and facilities to investors, but gave no investment guarantees.

The 1972 law was quite elaborate in the concessions provided investors, and the facilities and guarantees afforded. The concessions included exemption from the business profits tax for a period of five years, with the possibility of an additional five-year exemption if profits remained below a specified level; exemption from customs duties on machinery, equipment and spare parts for a period of five years; grant of land for buildings to be erected and used by new enterprises; rebate of customs and excise duties paid by a new enterprise on raw materials and packing materials; and free transfer abroad of profits and capital. In the case of capital transfer, this is to take place at the net value of the foreign captial invested in the enterprise upon liquidation.

The 1973 act aims at encouraging the investment of foreign capital in economic services in the Sudan with a view toward facilitating achievement of government plans to accelerate economic growth in the Sudan by granting concessions, facilities and guarantees.[14] Economic activities to be encouraged include tourism, transportation, warehousing, agricultural services, and any other activities that may help to develop the national economy as determined by the Minister of Finance and National Economy. Concessions under the 1973 Act include exemption from business profit taxes for periods ranging between three and six years, exemption from customs duties and fees, and the allotment of land at reduced price. Investors are given several types of guarantees including remittance abroad of all profits derived from the investment in the enterprise; in case of liquidation of an enterprise, transfer abroad of all imported capital originally registered with the Bank of Sudan; and protection against confiscation and nationalisation without reasonable compensation.

The act of 1974 replaced the legislation of 1972. The more recent legislation aims at encouraging investment in establishments (1) where raw material production will be promoted, (2) that shall provide employment opportunities, (3) whose production will reduce the need for importation, (4) where the aims of economic cooperation with Arab and African states will be furthered, and (5) that shall contribute to the increase in national income and national defence.

In general the 1974 act provides concessions that are similar to those included in the legislation two years earlier. New enterprises are afforded exemption from business profit taxes for a period of five years, with the possibility of an extension of five additional years for profits that remain within 10 per cent of capital. Exemptions are provided for customs duties paid on imports of machinery and spare parts.

Special facilities provisions permit reduced rates for electric power used by establishments, and reduced freight rates on machinery, equipment and raw materials. Additional provisions in the 1974 law relate to protection afforded local industries, guarantees against nationalisation and confiscation, and transfer of profits and capital abroad.

In addition to the various laws which have been designed to encourage foreign investment in the Sudan, consideration must be given to economic plans formulated by the government. Moreover, attention must be given to how specific foreign investment projects fit into realisation of economic planning targets. In general the economic plans of the 1970s are geared towards self-sufficiency in consumer goods production (sugar, textiles, and plastic sacks). While the contribution of the private sector to the industrial sphere of Sudan's economy is as yet not substantial, there is considerable opportunity for private enterprise including joint ventures between public and private sector firms. For example, the Plastic Sacks Company with a paid-up capital of £S.1,000,000 has 40 per cent public, 40 per cent foreign, and 20 per cent private Sudanese investment. The Kenanna Sugar Refinery has 49 per cent foreign and 51 per cent public investment. The mining and petroleum industries have a 50–50 division between public sector and private foreign investment. There remains considerable scope for foreign investment in industry in the Sudan. Priority is given to enterprises making use of the by-products of existing industries, such as in sugar refining (bagasse used for paper) and leather trimming.

E CONTRIBUTIONS, PAST, PRESENT AND FUTURE

It can be maintained that foreign trade and investment have made important contributions to the growth and prosperity of Sudan's economy. In the past the development of key export commodities has provided a base of foreign exchange earnings adequate to support merchandise import requirements, effect payments for services (shipping and insurance), and meet required external debt-servicing requirements. Foreign enterprise and investment were instrumental in developing the large irrigated areas that form the production base for commercially exportable commodities. Inward foreign investment and foreign loans have added to domestic capital formation, increased the ability to export, and permitted import-saving gains in output.

The magnitude of these contributions should not be overlooked. The Sudanese economy is only beginning to emerge from a boot-strap condition. The amount of domestic saving continues to represent a constraint on capital formation, growth in output, and ability to generate further exports.

In future the Sudanese economy may require greater proportionate contributions from the foreign sector. Whether these will be forthcoming will depend on a number of considerations. These include the degree of support and encouragement given to foreign investors by the government, the success of foreign trade and export policy, the availability of foreign investment funds, and the extent of success in domestic economic planning. In connection with this last point, it will be necessary for future economic plans to succeed in expanding the capacity to produce exportables at cost levels compatible with world trade price structure and to expand import-saving production as well.

The prospects for improved contributions through foreign trade and investment appear favourable. A significant increase in foreign investment appears likely, considering the proximity of the Sudan to the Middle East oil-exporting nations. Economic development requirements will call for enlarged investments by these oil-exporting nations in adjacent countries such as the Sudan to develop sources of supply for food, minerals, and low-cost labour-intensive manufactures (processed foods, textiles, and clothing). The Triad Investment Company, owned by Arab oil investors, has been actively searching for and evaluating investment and business opportunities in the Sudan.[15] It is believed that a significant amount of petrodollar investment will go into the Sudan to exploit its potential as a breadbasket for the oil-exporting nations. Such investment would make the Sudan an important exporter of foodstuffs, and could lead to the country following a pattern of export-led growth. Finally, a large inflow of foreign investment would permit agricultural and industrial development of an import-saving nature.

8 Development Planning: Problems and Prospects

A DEVELOPMENT PLANNING: GOAL FORMULATION AND PROBLEM AREAS

With close to two decades of political independence behind it, the Sudan has achieved much in the way of development progress despite significant obstacles and constraints. In that twenty-year period population has advanced by close to 75 per cent, the standard of living has improved for a significant part of the rural population, and urban areas have grown and prospered. Economic structure has shifted in the direction of increased industrial output, a more diversified export base, and relatively less dependence on traditional agriculture.

Government initiative has focused on development planning, a sizeable amount of state enterprise, and the provision of generous investment incentives. The Ten Year Plan of 1961–70 represents the first attempt at formulating and executing a comprehensive development plan for the Sudan. Major objectives of this Ten Year Plan included an increase in *per capita* income, broadened economic structure, export expansion and import substitution, and improved social conditions. The Ten Year Plan could be described as a collection of uncoordinated projects whose financing was provided for on a year-by-year basis. While production advances were significant both in agriculture and industry, the plan did not attain its basic objectives in the areas of *per capita* income, export expansion, and improved social conditions. However, modest achievements were accomplished in the direction of broadening the economic base.

In 1970 a Five Year Plan (1970–5) was initiated, also with ambitious objectives. Gross Domestic Product was targeted to expand at an annual rate of 8.1 per cent, gains in agricultural production were set at 77 per cent for the five-year period, while industrial output was to increase by 57 per cent. *Per capita* income was to increase by 31 per cent over the five-year period. Capital investment was scheduled to advance by 40 per cent in the public sector and 36 per cent in the private sector. The Five Year Plan was converted into a Seven Year Plan, which is described in a later section of this chapter. In general the Five Year Plan was not meeting its objectives. *Per capita* income remained largely stagnant throughout the early 1970s. Capital investment also fell behind due to lack of adequate financing and delay in completion of feasibility studies on a number of projects.

The inability of the Sudan to achieve development plan objectives would suggest that goal formulation has been somewhat less than scientific. Specific problems encountered in the first (Ten Year Plan of 1961–70) and second (Five Year Plan of 1970–5) plans are referred to in the following sections. Beyond this, we can find a more general set of problems that operate as a persistent negative factor in the Sudan. This focuses on the role of the government as a planning agency.

It is possible to identify six areas in which development planning by the central government has proven to be inefficient.[1] These may be summarised as follows:

1. Excessive political promises have led to overly ambitious development plans. As in many other African nations, the Sudanese look to the central government for improved social and economic conditions. Competition among political leaders for widespread popular support leads to declarations of policy objectives that tend to raise the level of expectations beyond that which is reasonably attainable. This process can lead to an escalation of state involvement in economic activity culminating in nationalisation of privately owned enterprises (as took place in the Sudan in 1970).

2. State activities become too extensive, overburden government machinery, and lead to public dissatisfaction. Government in the Sudan is not overly efficient. There continues to be a shortage of well-trained civil servants, and weak discipline with respect to government employees. Moreover, overextension of state activities tends to make people more dependent than is good for economic progress.

3. The government faces a problem of incomplete coordination between different agencies, and overlapping agency jurisdiction. With the increase in functions assumed by the state during the 1960s it has established a number of corporations, boards, councils, and committees. In 1970 there were at least eight major governmental units with the responsibility for dealing with agricultural problems and programmes. The same overlapping jurisdiction and resulting coordination problems exist in the fields of power and energy, and in industry.

4. In the Sudan there is a tendency to overprotect civil servants, and to avoid imposing discipline among employees of state organs. In part this is inherited from the British tradition of tenured security for government employees. In the Sudan it tends to be compounded by overstaffing in some departments, a condition that is not easily remedied in an underemployment economy.

5. State economic activities have performed poorly.[2] The railway has encountered sizeable operating losses. Inadequate transport services have prevented export of bulky agricultural products at peak periods. State-owned factories under the management of the Industrial Development Corporation have experienced financial losses due to inappropriate market studies and uncoordinated production and marketing.

6. Economic management has been poorly conceived and weakly administered. At times money supply growth has not been adequately checked in periods of inflation, wage increases have not been adequately held back to contain inflationary cost pressures, and the government has given in to strike action by employees and students. Beyond this, the government has assumed the task of regulating economic activities that are extremely difficult to control, e.g. price levels, exports, and the marketing of world-traded commodities (cotton and gum arabic). These difficulties are aggravated by a shortage of economic and business statistics, low literacy levels, inefficient state agencies, and a geographically widely scattered population.

B ECONOMIC DEVELOPMENT PLAN OF 1961–70

Development planning was initiated in the Sudan with two five-year programmes (1946–50 and 1950–5) covering the public sector. These pre-independence programmes were more in the nature of a list of investment proposals than a comprehensive and detailed analysis of the economy's needs and resources. Following independence interim efforts were devoted to preparation of national income estimates for the Sudan; assembly of detailed information relating to public sector investments; and construction of a macroeconomic framework with aggregated projections of income, fixed investment, finance sources, and balance of payments.[3] As a result of these efforts an initial seven-year plan was published early in 1962, which was subsequently extended to cover the ten-year period 1961–70.

The objectives of this plan were as follows:

(1) An increase in real *per capita* income with an ultimate objective of doubling per capita income within 25 years.
(2) Broadening the structure of the economy.

(3) Increasing exports and import substitution.
(4) Improvement in social conditions and creation of new employment opportunities.

These objectives were to be accomplished within an environment of relatively stable prices and balanced expansion of incomes and expenditures in the private and public sectors. Import substitution was to be achieved in the agricultural sector in the form of increased sugar and wheat production in the irrigated areas, and coffee and tea production in the southern provinces. Additional import substitution was to be derived from industrial development in textiles, footwear, sugar, cement and cigarettes.

The plan projected an overall growth rate of 5 per cent per annum. This represented growth rates of 6.7 per cent and 3.3 per cent per annum in the roughly equivalent modern and traditional sectors. These projected growth rates were overly ambitious in that they indicated high labour productivity improvements, and required a shift of 800,000 workers from the traditional to the modern sector.[4]

The plan called for a doubling of private gross fixed investment over the ten year period (average annual investment of £S.22.8 million). Public sector fixed investment was scheduled to increase moderately, and to make its major contribution to development through large scale gravity irrigation projects. Over 70 per cent of agricultural investment was designated for three major Nile irrigation projects including completion of the Managil extension to the Gezira, the first stage of construction of the Roseires Dam, and construction of a dam on the Atbara at Khasm el Girba. Of the modern sectors total gross fixed investment of £S.565 million during the ten-year period, £S.150 million was to be obtained from sources outside the Sudan.

Based on Wynn's analysis of the first six years of the ten-year plan, actual GDP came close to plan projections. However, after allowing for price level changes (an increase of 1.5 per cent per annum) the achieved growth was only three-fourths of the 6.7 per cent targeted for the modern sector. In this period capital outlays exceeded expectations, making the shortfall in real income growth even more serious. The greater than anticipated increase in investment came from a depletion of government cash reserves. Domestic and foreign savings failed to match investment and foreign exchange reserves declined. The central government's ordinary budget surpluses were not maintained, and persistent deficits appeared in the budgets of local governments and autonomous public agencies. The deterioration in government cash position together with an increase in commercial bank claims led to an excessive expansion in the money supply, which exceeded the overall growth rate of the economy. Rapid inflation was avoided largely because of an increased demand for money for transactions, and as a medium of savings in the traditional sector of the economy.

Agricultural expansion and investment resulted in significant gains in output, cultivated acreage, and application of modern agricultural methods. Completion of the Managil Extension brought the irrigated land in the Gezira-Managil Scheme to 2.1 million feddans. Use of mechanised equipment was increased. In the period 1961–73 the use of tractors increased from 2040 to 8000, and the number of combine harvesters in use increased from 120 to 700. Large-scale mechanised farming was introduced and expanded so that by 1974 2.4 million feddans were under cultivation by this method.

Efforts at broadening the industrial structure met with moderate success. While the percentages of GDP by industrial origin remained largely the same over the decade, there were noticeable gains in several new manufacturing sectors. The industrial sector made clearcut gains, especially in the later years of the decade. In the period 1966–9 cement, sugar, footwear, and textiles production increased by 93 per cent, 263 per cent, 49 per cent, and 27 per cent respectively.[5] In addition public-sector sugar and molasses factories at Khasm el Girba commenced production in 1965–6. These gains facilitated import substitution. Expansion of the irrigated sectors provided a broader base of middle-income-receiving families.

During the middle years of the decade it became apparent that financial disequilibrium was threatening success of the development plan. The imbalance was caused by large increases in central government budget expenditures and substantial deficits in the budgets of local and autonomous government bodies, unplanned investment, shortfalls in the expected level of foreign capital, and a larger than expected import bill on trade and invisibles. In 1963 the government response to this problem took the form of a freeze on filling government posts, rescheduled investments, increased import duties on consumer goods, and increases in profits tax and the introduction of an income tax. In 1964 commercial banks were asked to reduce advances to private sector businesses, and the government instituted a programme of intensified tax administration and collection. In 1966 and 1967 standby credits with the International Monetary Fund were linked with a mutually agreed upon stabilisation programme, including a restriction on bank advances.

The record suggests that important economic objectives of the ten-year plan were not realised. The economic growth rate was less than called for in the plan and there was no noticeable improvement in *per capita* income.[6] Moreover, financial equilibrium was not maintained. The reasons for failure to attain economic development objectives fall into three distinct categories. First, internal civil war in the 1960s vastly depleted the resources of the central government and overburdened the budget with defence and military expenditures. A comparison of military expenditures among African nations in the 1960s indicates that the Sudan ranks as one of the four highest in terms of military expenditures as a percentage of GNP and of government spending.[7] The split-off of the southern section of the nation resulted in a tremendous reversal in production and decline in economic well-being in the southern provinces. Second, the development plan incorrectly assessed the potential performance of the economy. For example, the incremental capital output ratio for the modern sector was 5-1 rather than the plan's estimated 4-1. In some cases plant construction has taken place without adequate provision for raw materials supplies. Infrastructure and industrial investment have been undertaken in the absence of forward and backward linkages and without adequate utilisation of by-products. Manufacturing has been expanded without appropriate consideration of distribution problems and the suitability of products to consumer demands.[8] Third, implementation of the plan left much to be desired. At times responsibility for the plan's execution was confused among several government departments. Strict budgetary control was not realised, and a maze of government bureaus and departments made it difficult to separately coordinate planning, controlling, and policy decision.

Nevertheless, significant gains were achieved. In light of the lack of experience and considering that the ten-year plan represented the first major development programme of the Sudan as an independent nation, the overall results are impressive. Agricultural output increased more rapidly than population and new products were introduced on a large-scale basis. Investment in agriculture permitted the expansion of irrigated acreage and the extension of mechanised agricultural methods. Finally, gains achieved in the manufacturing sector resulted in broadening the economic base and diversifying the domestic economy.

C ECONOMIC DEVELOPMENT PLAN OF 1971–7

The Five Year Industrial Development Plan (1970–5) of the Sudan succeeded the Ten Year Plan discussed in the preceding section. Prior to conclusion of this Five Year Plan it became a Seven Year Plan scheduled to be completed in 1977. The following discussion outlines the broad objectives of the Five Year Plan, and examines the Seven Year Plan in some detail.

On an overall basis the Five Year Plan (1970–5) was nearly as ambitious as its immediate predecessor. The plan provided for an annual increase in *per capita* income of 5.5 per cent and an expansion in industrial source GDP of 9.4 per cent annually (Table 8-1). Investment expenditures were scheduled to increase at an annual rate of 7.0 per cent.

TABLE 8-1 Basic Objectives of the Industrial Development Plan (1970–5)

	1969–70	*1974–5*	*Average annual increase* (%)
Total GDP/capita (US$)	104.5	136.7	5.5
Population (000)	15,500	17,500	2.5
Industrial GDP (US$)	145.9	229.8	9.4
Total GDP (US$ m.)	1,620.0	2,392.4	8.1
Industry % of total GDP	9.0	9.6	
Investment (US$ m.)*	756.8	1,062.6	7.0
Exports (US$ m.)	307.6	518.8	11.1
Employment (000)	8,620	9,570	2.1

* Figures reflect five-year total, period ending on designated year.
SOURCE UNIDO, *Summaries of Industrial Development Plans*, Volume III (1973), p. 336.

Broader objectives of the Five Year Plan included increased government revenues, a 77 per cent expansion in agricultural source GDP, an increase in livestock production of over 75 per cent, a broadened base of industrial products, development of urban and rural power networks, to provide all cities and villages with electricity and drinking water, and to guarantee full employment.[9]

Details of the Seven Year Interim Programme of Action were released by the Sudanese government in 1972, with the intent of having the terminal year of the Seven Year Plan coincide with the final year of office of President Nimeiri.[10] A basic objective of the Seven Year Plan is to achieve self-sufficiency in essential goods and services, to achieve better balance between production and consumption, and to minimise the burden on the economy of government budgetary expenses.

The first sector of the Sudan economy considered in the published plan is agriculture. A number of priorities are established in agricultural development including (1) improved efficiency in existing projects, (2) attainment of self-sufficiency in all imported agricultural products that comprise 50 per cent of all Sudanese imports, (3) surplus production for export, (4) diversification of agricultural production, and (5) regional integration of agricultural production. The plan calls for attainment of self-sufficiency in wheat, cotton textiles, sugar, rice, coffee, tobacco, kenaf, and paper. The concept of regional integration includes expanded production in southern and western provinces with shipment of their surpluses to other areas of the country, and more intensified use of areas of the country presently under-utilised for agriculture (Northern Province and Kassala).

A second part of the Seven Year Plan establishes priorities in the development of irrigation and hydroelectric power. These include improvements in existing irrigation services, increased utilisation of Sudan's share of the Nile waters (the Sudan is now using 12 of the 18.5 milliard cubic metres annual allowance under the agreement established with Egypt),[11] development of other water resources in various parts of the Sudan, and provision of additional hydroelectric power for industrial and general consumption.[12] Irrigation projects already in process or under planning include the Northwestern Sennar Project wherein a 37,000-feddan area has been irrigated for sugar production, the Rehad Project providing 300,000 feddans of pump irrigation, redevelopment of the Sennar Dam with a rebuilt sluice, a Kenaf Project in Blue Nile Province, changing Northern Province Projects from flooding to gravity irrigation, an increase in the wheat-planted area in the Gezira and Managil extension, and agricultural reform projects designed to increase productivity by electrification, reorganisation of land use and improved management practices.

In industry and mining, priorities include self-sufficiency in basic consumption areas, development of traditional and handicraft industries to lessen the drift of population from rural to urban areas, utilisation of local raw materials in industry, and improvement of the geographic distribution of industries throughout the Sudan. Four programme areas are specified in the Seven Year Programme to promote industrial development. These aim at self-sufficiency in basic manufacturing products (sugar, textiles, wheat flour, cigarettes, paper, and (kenaf) sacks); development of export trade in hides and leather, textiles, canned fruit, sugar, and sacks; to train semi-skilled manpower; and to better integrate processing industries with agricultural production.

A fourth part of the Seven Year Plan focuses on domestic and international trade. Internal self-sufficiency programmes are described by commodity category. Export objectives are detailed by commodity and attention is given to the means and channels of communication available for furthering foreign trade.

A fifth aspect of the Seven Year Plan details the priorities and programmes for improvement of transportation and communication. Priorities include increasing the efficiency of transport and communications, development of closer connections between producing and consuming regions, reduction of travel costs, and improved postal and telephone connections with the rest of the world. The transport and communication area is given more detailed attention than any other in the Seven Year Plan, reflecting the considerable lag in infrastructure development in the Sudan. Table 8-2 summarizes the types of development targets established.

TABLE 8-2 Transport and Communication Development Targets, Seven Year Plan (1971–7)

Sector	*Projects*
A Road extensions.	1. To complete road from Kosti-Sennar to Malakal and Juba.
	2. To construct Port Sudan–Khartoum highway via Kassala, Gedaref and Medani.
	3. To construct Gedaref–Daka–Gelabat road.
	4. To construct Nyala–Zalingi road.
	5. To construct Dubeibat–Dilling–Kadugli road.
	6. To carry out road construction connecting Sudan with neighbouring African countries according to bilateral agreements and the Organisation for African Union.
	7. To complete the feasibility studies for northern roads linking Sudan with Libya and Egypt.
B Bridges across Nile and tributaries.	1. White Nile bridge at Kosti.
	2. Elrigaf Bridge at Juba.
	3. Bridge over River Jur.
	4. Bridge Atbara River.
C Airport modernisation.	1. Construction of new Khartoum Airport.
	2. Asphalting runways of major airports and technical modernisation.
	3. Deveop and modernise Juba and Port Sudan airports to be international alternative airports.
D River and sea line transport.	1. To develop river transport to make it assume greater role in internal commerce. This would be accomplished by acquisition of new steamers, clearing waterways and erecting navigation signs, expansion of Juba and Kosti navigation workshops, to establish new routes between Khartoum and Atbara, Sennar, and Kosti, and provision of loading machines.
	2. To improve facilities for shipping exports and imports at Red Sea port.
	3. To connect with Far East with regular shipping line.

TABLE 8-2—(cont.)

Sector	*Projects*
E Mechanical transport.	Decentralisation: 1. Establish workshops and stores in all provincial capitals. 2. Expand and consolidate existing workshops. 3. Improve on stores and loaders. 4. Expand gas stations. 5. Establish a school for mechanical transport training. 6. Build residences for employees and labourers in remote areas.
F Sudan airways.	1. Replace old planes with modern aircraft. 2. To increase transport of goods. 3. To expand internal and international lines. 4. Maintain better services and training.
G Railways.	1. To provide stations with direct telephone and electronic equipment. 2. To use quick means for inspection (helicopter). 3. To convert from steam to diesel locomotives. 4. To expand Port Sudan port and build new port south of Port Sudan. 5. To rebuild Khartoum Station. 6. To build switching facilities in Port Sudan. 7. To complete studies to carry out railway project linking Sudan with Chad, Egypt and Central African Republic.
H Postal and telegraph service	1. To cover whole area of the Sudan with service. 2. Improve services: (a) have Post Office for every 6000 people. (b) make P.O. boxes in streets and use home delivery. (c) increase use of mobile post cars in Kordofan, Darfur, and Blue Nile Provinces. (d) provide additional vehicles for big city use, and provide inspection vehicles. 3. Provide telegraph service for all Post offices. 4. Provide automatic telex circuits in Port Sudan, Atbara, Modani, and El Obeid. 5. Make telex kiosks in hotels and various offices. 6. Use phone in dictating telegrams before sending them.

Natural resource development represents the sixth and final major area covered in the Seven Year Plan. Natural resources includes water development, forestry, and rural development. Programmes for ground water and surface water include drilling and maintenance of wells, expansion of record stations for big wadis, feasibility study of providing drinking water for big towns using wadis, and construction of dams and reservoirs to make better use of surface water and wadis. Forestry development programmes include development of *acacia senegal* forests and expanded tapping of acacia to raise production by 2500 tons (gum arabic) annually, feasibility studies for reserve forests, development of forestry in desert areas, and continued research for improved use of forest potential. The rural development phase of the Seven Year Plan provides for cooperation with various specialised institutions to promote rural development, settlement of nomads, and development of the Abezi Area as a model for future cultural integration in the north and south.

The Seven Year Plan is detailed as well as comprehensive. In contrast to the earlier Ten Year Plan there is considerable scope within the plan for feasibility studies, which would form the basis of further project evaluation and programme structuring.

D EVALUATION

Development planning in the Sudan has as its objective attainment of a maximum level of investment expenditure consonant with efficiency in its sectoral and regional allocation. To accomplish this the plan must satisfy the following two conditions:

1. Consider the major constraints that work against a high level of investment and economic development.
2. Structure plan objectives and priorities that are suitable to the stage of industrial development of the Sudan.

1 *Investment Constraints*

Over the past two decades four types of constraints have tended to slow investment and economic advance in the Sudan. The relative importance of these constraints has varied from one period of time to the next. The four major constraints, which include the investment climate, infrastructure, absorptive capacity, and foreign exchange, are depicted in Table 8-3. Their relative importance is indicated by a numerical ordering of 1 through 4 (1 represents the highest order of constraint).

In the five-year period immediately following independence (1956–60) lack of infrastructure posed the most serious problem for the Sudan. The need to invest in infrastructure placed a strain on extremely limited foreign exchange earnings, at that time the second

TABLE 8-3 Changing Investment Constraints in the Sudan, 1956–80

Type investment constraint	1956–60	1961–5	1966–70	1971–5	1976–80
Investment Climate: receptiveness of government to private foreign investment.	4	4	1	1–4	nil
Infrastructure: availability of fixed capital including roads, other transportation, electric power.	1	1	3	2–1	1
Absorptive Capacity: ability of local economy to productively utilise new additions to the capital stock.	3	2	4	4–2	2
Foreign Exchange: availability affected by amount and growth of current earnings, and need to use current earnings for imports and debt service.	2	3	2	3–4	nil

NOTE Numbers 1–4 indicate ordinal ranking of constraint. No. 1 indicates most severe constraint, and No. 4 indicates least severe constraint.

most significant constraint. In the second five-year period (1961–5) foreign exchange became a less critical problem area as large inward capital movements took place. For example, in 1961 investment in the Sudan American Textile Industry attracted £S.4.3 million, and in 1964 the Shell Oil Company refinery at Port Sudan brought £S.1.3 million of equipment investments into the country. In the period 1961–5 gross foreign private capital investment in the Sudan was £S.14.2 million and net foreign private capital investment was £S.12.5 million.[13] This fails to consider public investment (World Bank loans, intergovernmental transfers, etc.). Balance of payments data indicate an average annual capital inflow in this five year period of £S.14.6 million.[14] This represents 7.4 per cent of average annual GDP in this period.[15]

The third period (1966–70) was characterised by civil war, economic slowdowns, and a reversal in the investment climate. Hallett notes that this period was filled with political changes and a tendency toward political divisiveness, even in the northern half of the Sudan.[16] In 1970 the government carried out general nationalisation and expropriations. Given the poor investment climate, the flow of foreign capital dried up. The fourth period (1971–5), which recently ended, was transitional. A turnaround was effected with amicable settlement of the southern question, and the investment incentives legislation of 1972–4 and efforts of the government to provide reasonable settlement to private investors has improved the investment climate. Moreover, the availability of substantial investment funds by Kuwaiti and Saudi Arabian investment banks has reduced the foreign exchange constraint. Given the continuation of a pro-foreign investment policy by the Sudanese government and the availability of generous amounts of OPEC investment funds, the investment climate and foreign exchange constraints become nil.[17] Under these conditions the significant limits to investment and economic advance become infrastructure and absorptive capacity.

2 *Transitional Stages and Policy*

Development planning, related investment incentives legislation, and economic policy in the Sudan must be evaluated in connection with the economic development status of the country and within the framework of overall government needs and policies aimed at promoting industrial development. The government policy mix should include complementary features that do not unduly distort economic incentives and relationships, and that are realistic in light of real world economic conditions.

In Table 8-4 we have depicted 'Transitional Stages in Sudanese Development'. In the first column the stage is depicted along with the chronology of years in which the particular stage manifests itself. The second column depicts the status of agricultural activity. The third column depicts the status of manufacturing activity and employment. Columns four and five describe the savings and finance and the balance of payments situations, respectively. The final column characterises the government policy mix and provides specific details on its implementation. The objective in constructing this table is to more clearly visualise the appropriateness (or lack) of government policy given general economic and financial conditions in the Sudan at that time. In part the table is designed to respond to the question 'Are fiscal incentives or foreign trade controls a more useful approach toward fostering industrial development in a less developed country?'

TABLE 8-4 Transitional Stages in Sudanese Development

Stage	*Agriculture*	*Manufacturing and employment*	*Domestic saving and finance*	*Balance of payments*	*Government policy mix*
1. Pre-industrial (period up to 1965)	Extension of modern agricultural methods to selected projects	Limited industrial activity. Industrial output under 5% of GDP. Little employment in manufacturing.	Limited saving, under 10% GDP. Early stage of bank growth. Expatriate banks important.	Deficit in trade. Surplus on capital. Light external debt service burden.	'Agricultural expansion and new processing industries. Investment incentives. Protective duties are high. Export duties.
2. Emerging industrial (1965 to 1985)	Expansion of modern cultivated area. Development of related processing industries. Import substitution. Reallocation of land and other resources to higher priority. Restoration of southern agriculture.	Industrial output expanding rapidly. Approx. 10% GDP. Employment in manufacturing growing rapidly.	Moderate savings. Banking sector expanding more rapidly than GDP.	Small trade deficit. Surplus on capital. Substantial external debt service.	'Consumer goods self-sufficiency'. Import substitution. Investment incentives (primarily fiscal). Shift in composition of tax revenues.
3. Moderate industrial development (1985–?)	Modern agric. methods used in all parts of country. Expansion of commercial agric. for exports.	Industrial diversification taking place. Industrial output now 15% of GDP. Manuf. employ 4–5% of total.	Savings adequate to finance internal investment needs. Financial institution diversification.	Balanced trade account. Borrowing from overseas to achieve foreign exchange balance. Large external debt service.	'Unified domestic markets to achieve scale economies'. Income and profits tax subsidies to industries. Export incentives.

The answer is that it all depends, in part on the stage of industrial development of the country.[18]

In the period up to 1965 the Sudan could be described as in a 'pre-industrial' stage of development, characterised by limited application of modern agriculture, limited industrial activity, practically no opportunity for employment in manufacturing industry, limited domestic savings, a tendency toward foreign trade deficit, and the need to import capital (Table 8-4). In this period the major thrust of government policy was to expand agricultural output and initiate new processing industries. In 1956, with the attainment of political independence, Sudan enacted an Approved Enterprises Law and in the absence of an internal tax base resorted to relatively high levels of import and export duties to raise revenue and encourage industrial enterprises.

At present the Sudan is in a second transitional stage of industrialisation. In the 'emerging industrial' stage agriculture continues to expand at a moderate pace, and manufacturing production is growing at a rapid pace but only in narrow lines of product categories. Therefore beneficial externality effects are limited. Industrial output represents approximately 10 per cent of GDP and employment in manufacturing is absorbing a larger proportion of the workforce than it did in the previous stage. Rising incomes in the manufacturing and service-related labour force generates increased savings, and as a result deposits and assets in the banking sector are expanding more rapidly than GDP. In this stage, the Sudan is utilising a wide range of foreign sources of capital funds. In this stage government policy aims at consumer goods self-sufficiency and in connection with this heavy emphasis is given to import substitution policies.

In this second stage an appropriate policy mix is needed to encourage more efficient agriculture, and to stimulate manufacturing activities that fit into the economic structure of the Sudan. The Sudan appears to possess natural advantages in the food processing and materials refining industry sectors, and these are the sectors that the government has given high priority to in its seven year (1971–7) development plan. The government is applying a combination of foreign trade (import substitution) and internal fiscal measures. The fiscal measures include tax relief and site subsidies. At present the Sudan is not in a position to generate a high proportion of tax revenues from income or direct taxes. However, this is gradually changing. The current need for foreign trade sources of tax revenues results in a blending of import substitution and fiscal incentives to promote industrialisation. While it can be argued that less distortion in domestic resource allocation might take place by greater use of direct fiscal incentives and less use of import duties, it will be some time before the domestic tax system is strong enough to generate the resources required to finance domestic industrial subsidies on a significant scale.[19]

Reasonable success could place the Sudan in a third stage, 'moderate industrial development', as early as 1985. At this point the economy would be moving toward industrial diversification, with a wider range of industrial production more evenly spread over all geographical regions. In this stage industrial product would account for over 15 per cent of GDP and employment in manufacturing would encompass 5 per cent or more of the labour force. Domestic saving, financial institution diversification, a more balanced foreign trade, and a broader base of tax revenues would characterise the economy. In this stage the government would aim at greater unification of domestic markets to achieve scale economies in manufacturing.

It should be noted that the appropriate policy mix changes over the course of these transitional stages. An appropriate policy mix in the first stage may be inappropriate in the second stage. With respect to experience in the Sudan, during stage one (1956–60) fiscal incentives could not be highly productive in stimulating investment due to (*a*) lack of a well developed fiscal or tax system, (*b*) lack of infrastructure, and (*c*) need to apply relatively high taxes on foreign trade due to lack of an alternative tax base. Therefore, foreign trade control measures (including import substitution) had to be relied on. In the second stage a more fully developed fiscal system has been developed and there exists greater opportunity to make use of fiscal incentives to encourage industrial investment. In the third stage we can anticipate even less reliance on foreign trade control measures as a widened internal market permits domestic producers to reap the benefits of large-scale production.

9 Balanced Regional Progress in the Future

The Sudan may be characterised as consisting of a small number of semi-modern towns and cities surrounded by vast areas of rural traditionalism and backwardness. One of the major challenges for future progress in the Sudan lies in this geographical isolation of many of its communities. The territorial vastness of the Sudan and its widespread arid areas operate as constant barriers to integration of the more modernised communities.

In the future an important aspect of development progress in the Sudan will consist of overcoming this tendency toward geographic fragmentation. Integration of the modern sector will require progress along physical, economic, social and organisational lines. This will necessitate coordinated programming to achieve integrated rural development, improved transport, and balance in progress achieved between town and rural areas. One criticism (not fully justified) that has been levelled at Sudanese development policy is that efforts have been overly restricted to a narrow sector of the national economy, e.g., the Khartoum–Gezira central area. This and other questions pertaining to centralised versus decentralised development patterns are discussed in some detail in the following sections.

A CENTRALIST TENDENCIES

1 *Centralist Tendencies in the Sudan*

The past two decades have witnessed a pattern of economic development in the Sudan where most of the gains have been concentrated in a central area which may be referred to as 'the Khartoum conurbation'. This embraces a circular land area that would have a radius of approximately 100 miles with its midpoint at Khartoum.

A number of factors have influenced this centralist pattern of development. In 1964 the United Nations study of population and manpower in the Sudan commented on the relatively sparse population, noting that it served as a 'hindrance to many types of developmental efforts'.[1] For example, low population density translates into high *per capita* costs where road and railway extensions and educational and medical-health services are provided. In addition, the population of the Sudan is poorly distributed. This results in a concentration of efforts within areas 'which offer the greatest advantages'. In short, the existing population density and distribution and prospective changes in these areas are important considerations in shaping development policy and strategy.

The importance and strategic role of government policy also contributes to a centralist development pattern. In the Sudan, as in many other developing countries, the government enjoys a key role in economic planning and in the development process in general. The national government requires a staff of decision-makers and researchers located at one central location. Since this group is influential in determining the level and direction of the nations economic activities, businessmen and other interested parties prefer to locate in close proximity. Poor transport and communications facilities outside the capital city make this location more desirable and in some cases imperative. Once the tendency for centralisation of activities is established it becomes self-reinforcing. Availability of scale and external economies reinforce this process.

Finally, there is evidence to support the view that taxation-spending patterns have resulted in subsidising urban industrial sectors at the expense of rural agricultural sectors. This results from the relatively heavy tax burden imposed on commodities, including export duties on agricultural products. It further stems from the high priorities given to machinery and equipment imports, and the protection accorded new manufacturing industries in the Sudan. In comparison with other developing countries, the extent of this redistributional effect in the Sudan is probably minimal. This is due to the priority given in the Sudan to extensive agricultural development, taking the form of imported farm equipment, subsidies to irrigation projects, and investment in transportation infrastructure required to facilitate movement of agricultural products to domestic and export markets.

2 *Urbanism*

Urbanism is one manifestation of centralist tendencies.[2] While urban population growth in the Sudan has outdistanced rural population growth (Table 9-1), a relatively small percentage of the total population (13.2 per cent in 1975) resides in urban area. Projections

TABLE 9-1 Urbanisation Patterns in a Sample of Less Developed Countries

Country	Per capita GNP level in 1972 (US$)	Population ('000s) 1975 Urban	Population ('000s) 1975 Rural	Population ('000s) 2000 Urban	Population ('000s) 2000 Rural	% of urban population 1975	% of urban population 2000	Compound urban growth rate 1970–5	Compound urban growth rate 1995–2000	Compound rural growth rate 1970–5	Compound rural growth rate 1995–2000
Type I											
Argentina	1,290	20,293	5,091	29,288	3,573	79.9	89.1	2.19	1.11	−2.46	−1.66
Mexico	750	37,349	21,855	103,287	28,957	63.1	78.1	4.86	3.60	1.19	0.82
Colombia	400	15,938	9,952	40,115	11,349	61.6	78.0	5.24	2.96	2.58	0.13
Brazil	530	65,128	44,602	161,604	50,903	59.4	76.1	4.72	3.13	1.67	0.31
Type II											
Algeria	430	8,432	8,455	27,205	11,199	49.9	70.8	6.78	3.85	1.52	0.94
Egypt	240	17,822	19,546	42,716	23,726	47.7	64.3	4.20	3.24	1.15	0.49
Korea	310	16,074	17,875	36,019	15,979	47.4	69.3	6.66	2.26	−1.36	−0.68
Philippines	220	15,837	29,468	46,068	47,956	35.0	49.0	4.25	3.66	3.02	0.99
Malaysia	430	3,641	8,666	9,888	12,589	29.6	44.0	3.34	3.28	2.09	0.58
Type III											
Senegal	260	1,262	3,190	3,740	5,013	28.4	42.7	3.89	4.18	1.83	1.47
Ivory Coast	340	994	3,891	3,718	5,899	20.4	38.7	7.02	4.46	1.51	1.54
Nigeria	130	11,419	51,511	40,953	94,008	18.2	30.3	4.67	5.10	2.07	2.36
Sudan	120	2,400	15,782	9,438	31,704	13.2	22.9	6.10	5.43	2.57	2.69
Kenya	170	1,483	11,625	6,458	24,743	11.3	20.7	6.48	5.61	3.38	2.83
Upper Volta	70	502	5,556	1,827	9.828	8.3	15.7	5.01	4.87	1.84	2.10
Type IV											
Pakistan	130	18,939	53,418	65,357	93,170	26.2	41.2	4.45	4.28	2.42	1.53
India	110	132,367	488,742	354,872	748,834	21.3	32.2	3.62	3.92	2.09	1.27
Indonesia	90	26,232	110,284	78,433	171,519	19.2	31.4	4.54	4.01	2.32	1.29
China (mainland)	170	207,510	630,406	478,404	673,555	24.8	41.5	4.31	2.75	0.84	−0.07

SOURCE International Bank for Reconstruction and Development, *The Task Ahead for the Cities of the Developing Countries*, Bank Staff Working Paper No. 209, July 1975, p. 7.

of the World Bank study group indicate that in the year 2000 urban population will be between one-fourth and one-fifth of total population.

Nations that have increased their *per capita* incomes and productivity have become increasingly more urban. This is reflected in Table 9-1. According to this analysis Type I countries enjoy relatively high incomes and have between one-half and three-fourths of their population living in urban areas. Type II countries enjoy somewhat lower incomes and have a smaller proportion of their population living in urban areas. Type IV countries include low income countries with severe land pressures. Type III countries, which include the Sudan, are predominately rural but are urbanising at a fairly rapid rate. Income differentials have stimulated large rural-to-urban population migrations, but land remains relatively abundant and agricultural development offers the opportunity to absorb larger numbers of people with continued gains in productivity. Type III countries such as the Sudan possess the ability to determine the pattern of urban growth over the next several decades through policies that affect location costs and opportunities of the manufacturing and service industry sectors. The present relatively small size of urban population in the Sudan makes the question of urban growth more manageable than in other countries where a higher percentage of urban population has become a pattern of living.

3 *Advantages of Centralist Tendencies*

It has been well expressed by Hirschman that an economy must develop one or more regional centres or 'growth poles' to be able to initiate economic progress leading to higher income levels.[3] Once these growth-impelled centres exist, development energies will be transmitted to adjacent outlying areas. In short, the development of growth centres can be viewed as a precondition for the development process itself. Once these centres have appeared, government policy can be directed toward adjustment of the degree and content of centralist tendency development.

Moderate centralist development tendencies in the Sudan have exerted beneficial effects in a number of connections. First, development of the Khartoum–Gezira and Port Sudan areas has permitted the absorption of workers previously underemployed in the traditional sector. This shift of manpower toward higher-productivity and higher-income occupations is an integral part of the development process.

A second contribution lies in the provision of income-supplementing employment opportunities to rural workers on a seasonal basis. We have already referred to the large numbers of seasonal workers that find employment in the centrally located irrigated and mechanised agricultural areas in the Sudan. For the most part these workers migrate from rural areas where employment and income-earning opportunities are less attractive and supplement their earnings from traditional agricultural activities or other occupational pursuits. In many cases these workers migrate long distances to secure temporary seasonal employment, which reflects substantial regional earnings differentials.

Another contribution from centralised development in the Sudan is in the outlet provided for agricultural output via increased domestic (urban) markets and more efficient processing facilities located in the more modern manufacturing centers. While the Sudan has experienced some difficulties in establishing agricultural processing plants (sugar, kenaf, canning, milk, and onion dehydration), the country has reached a point where farm producers are no longer totally dependent on the vagaries of market conditions at the point in time when the product is harvested.

The Sudan is and will continue to be short of skilled and technically trained manpower. For this reason, it is highly advantageous to have a centralised labour market and pool of labour so that this scarce resource can be put to work most effectively and with a minimum of frictional lag. Only after the Sudan has developed a significantly larger pool of skilled and technically trained labour could it afford the luxury of decentralised development and a number of development 'nodes', each supported by its own pool of highly trained manpower.

Finally, we should note that the Sudan is not quite ready for a high degree of decentralised development. The country lacks effective means of transportation. Given this shortcoming, decentralised development would require that each region or development node move ahead on a non-integrated basis. This non-integrated regional development would persist until transport infrastructure could 'catch up'.

B DISPERSIONIST TENDENCIES

1 *Need for Rural Development*

The central governments of African nations are aware that the social and political problems reflected in regional income disparities within their borders represent a potential source of instability. Such imbalances in income distribution constitute a barrier to peaceful progress toward development. In the Sudan as in other developing African nations considerations of social policy involving value judgements play an important role in determining the proper policy mix as between centralist and dispersionist development programming.

A strong argument can be made for placing greater emphasis in the future on rural development (dispersionist development planning) in the Sudan. Increased job opportunities in rural areas would lessen pressures on urban job markets caused by in-migration of those seeking employment. Income disparities between urban and rural areas would be narrowed. Infrastructure and welfare requirements would be minimised since associated costs generally are lower in rural as compared with urban areas and because lower standards can be more easily accepted in rural areas.[4]

Urban areas almost automatically are better able to compete for people, investment funds, and productive resources than rural areas. This is because governments fail to charge urban households and business firms the full social costs associated with their operations (including pollution, noise, and congestion). Concentrated political power tends to produce a favoured position for big cities in the allocation of development planning and command over productive resources. This view sees urban growth as based on exploitation of a rural surplus. High and rising expenditures for urban transport, housing and welfare are viewed as an excessive and wasteful practice. Such amenities can be better provided in rural regions at lower cost.

2 *Rural Growth Centres*

Rural development would focus on those strengths and comparative advantage opportunities that best suit the Sudan. There can be no doubt that in future agricultural development will represent the major source of increased employment and income-gaining opportunities in the Sudan. The major barriers to this development are (1) lack of infrastructure (especially transport and power), and (2) availability of investment funds and domestic savings to finance investment in more productive modern sector agriculture.

In addition, rural development requires the establishment of regional and local growth centres. In this way activities that otherwise gravitate to urban centres, leaving rural areas without such services, would become rooted in these newly developing rural development centres. This approach would require formulating a medium-term regional capital budget for rural centres in each of the regions of the country.[5]

C POLICY APPROACHES AND STRATEGIES

Policies for rural development should be two-pronged, namely to expand employment opportunites in agriculture and to reduce the number of underemployed and unemployed through the establishment of nonfarm employment opportunities. Measures should include diversification by creating of agro-industrial activities. Potential resource regions should be identified. These regions would include untapped or underutilised resources. Selection of these resource regions for special treatment would follow analysis of alternative resource use and potential interregional effects. The following criteria have been suggested as applicable in an analysis of this type.[6]

(1) permanent settlement
(2) acceleration of regional growth rate
(3) increased productivity
(4) generation of employment opportunities
(5) promotion of better housing and sanitation conditions
(6) development of exports
(7) minimisation of inputs.

Special consideration will have to be given to areas of structural poverty. Moreover, a system of regional centres or development nodes would have to be delineated. These would function as focal points for public and private investments as well as integrated social overhead projects. A hierarchy of these rural centres could be established whereby lower-ranking centres perform basic services and higher-ranking centres perform basic plus more specialised services. Each growth centre would become a hub from which would radiate a network of all-weather and seasonal roads. Existing provincial capitals would form the higher-ranking centres. Other towns and settlements would be categorised as lower ranking centres. A programme would be established where each growth point would receive an implantation of service-oriented facilities (government administration, education, light industry, health and medical, agricultural extension, and cultural).

In executing this approach, numerous planning tasks will become necessary. These will include creation of a network of interdependent regions that encompass the whole country, identification of inconsistencies in the economic and social structures of primary economic regions, comparison of actual regional output with potential output as indicated by factor endowments of that region, and establishment and maintenance of a comprehensive data base with indices of regional and national economic performance.

Notes

CHAPTER 1

1. S. Longrigg, *The Middle East, A Social Geography* (Chicago: Aldine Publishing Co., 1963) p. 103.
2. Mountjoy, and Embleton, *Africa*: *A New Geographical Survey* (New York: Praeger, 1967) p. 318.
3. Walter Fitzgerald, *Africa*: *A Social, Economic and Political Geography of its Major Regions* (London: Methuen, 1952) p. 422.
4. Harrison Church, *Africa and the Islands* (New York: Wiley, 1964) p. 176.
5. B. G. Haycock, 'The Impact of Meroitic and Nubian Civilizations on Africa, in *Sudan in Africa* by Yusuf Fadi Hasan (Khartoum: Khartoum University Press, 1971) p. 38.
6. A. J. Arkell, *History of the Sudan* (London: University of London, The Athlone Press, 1961) p. 110.
7. Y. F. Hassan, *The Arabs and the Sudan* (Khartoum: Khartoum University Press, 1973).
8. Sir Douglas Newbold, *The Making of the Modern Sudan* (Conn.: Greenwood Press, 1974) p. 481.
9. Arkell, p. 225.
10. P. M. Holt, *A Modern History of the Sudan* (New York: Grove Press, 1961) p. 77.
11. Holt, p. 122.
12. Ibrahim, Hassan Ahmed, 'The Sudan in the Anglo-Egyptian Treaty', *Sudan Notes and Records*, Vol. LIV (1973) p. 13.
13. Mohamed O. Beshir, *The Southern Sudan*: *Background to Conflict* (Khartoum: Khartoum University Press, 1970) p. 39.
14. M. O. Besher, *The Southern Sudan*: *Background to Conflict* (Khartoum: Khartoum University Press, 1970) p. 61.
15. Ali A. Mazuri, *The Multiple Marginality of the Sudan in Africa,* First International Conference, February 1968 (Khartoum: Khartoum University Press, 1971).
16. Ministry of Industry and Mining, Government Printer, *Mining and Oil Exploration Laws in the Sudan* (Khartoum, 1974) p. 87.
17. This was in connection with the flooding of areas resulting from construction of the Aswan Dam.

18. W. David Hopper, 'The Development of Agriculture in Developing Countries', *Scientific American*, September 1976, p. 197.

CHAPTER 2

1. This figure excludes approximately one million cattle-herding nomads who move in response to variations in rainfall. The question of what constitutes a nomad poses real problems for census-takers and analysts of labour market developments. See United Nations, *Population Growth and Manpower in the Sudan*, A Joint Study by the United Nations and Government of the Sudan, Population Studies No. 37 (New York, 1964) pp. 139–40.
2. The ease with which these migrant workers find jobs reflects a relatively efficient labour market. This may appear surprising for a country such as the Sudan with a poorly developed transport system and lack of good communications regarding work opportunities.
3. International Labour Office, *Growth, Employment and Equity, A Comprehensive Strategy for Sudan* (first report of the ILO/UNDP employment mission, 1975) Volume I, October 1975, IIIC, p. 2.
4. Approximately 876,000 reside in the Khartoum area out of an urban population of 2,487,000.
5. Gabal al Din and Mohamed El Awad, 'The Factors Influencing Migration to the Three Towns of the Sudan', *Sudan Journal of Economic and Social Studies*, Vol. I, No. 1, summer 1974. Also O. Okereke, 'Migrant Labour and its Economic Implication to African Agriculture', *Eastern Africa Journal of Rural Development*, 1975, pp. 95–6. United Nations, *Population Growth and Manpower in the Sudan*, 1964, p. 57.
7. In many cases housewives are highly productive workers. For example, housewives may provide a major part of the agricultural labour on family-operated farms, especially at times when the husband moves to another location to take seasonal employment.
8. United Nations, *Population Growth and Manpower in the Sudan*, 1964, pp. 57 and 145.
9. One of the aims of government policy is to reduce income and employment inequalities among the provinces. Consequently, a programme for special assistance to the southern provinces is operated through the Southern Regional Fund which in 1974–5 was budgeted for £S.12 million.
10. United Nations, *Population Growth and Manpower in the Sudan*, 1964, p. 67.
11. It should be noted that in organised sectors additional payments are made which are not necessarily reflected in the survey data. These include attendance and incentive bonuses, subsidised lunch, medical care, free transport or transport allowance, housing loans, and recreational facilities.
12. ILO, *Employment, Incomes and Equality: A Strategy for Increasing Productive Employment in Kenya* (Geneva, 1973).
13. In 1974 there were 96,000 tenant families in the Gezira.
14. In connection with cotton picking in the Gezira some 65,000 local workers are employed for this purpose.

15. The number of migrant workers employed in the Gezira on a seasonal basis for cotton-picking exceeds 320,000.
16. Mechanised farms generally have 1000 or more feddans of which one-third is kept fallow.
17. Under the Sudan Trade Unions Ordinance of 1949 any ten persons could organise a trade union and register it.
18. Abdel–Rahman E. Ali Taha, *Labour Relations in the Sudan* (University of Khartoum Press, 1975) p. 18.

CHAPTER 3

1. UNIDO, *Industrial Development Survey*, Special Issue for the Second General Conference of UNIDO at Lima, Peru, March 12–26, 1975 (New York: United Nations, 1974, pp. 260–1.
2. The economic plan for the ten-year period was to increase GDP by 8.1 per cent annually. In reality a growth of 4.7 per cent annually was realised. See *Sudan Today* (University Press of Africa, 1971), pp. 68–9 for description of the progress achieved in this decade.
3. While most of the active population is engaged in agricultural pursuits, only 40 per cent of gross domestic product is derived from agriculture. This results from the low average productivity per worker in agriculture.
4. Omar Osman and A. A. Suleiman, 'The Economy of the Sudan', in Robson and Lury, *The Economies of Africa* (George Allen & Unwin, 1969), p. 439.
5. In the period 1955–67 the modern sector increased in importance as a contributor to GDP. In 1955–7 the modern sector accounted for 45 per cent of output, but by 1965–7 accounted for 49 per cent of the total.
6. UNIDO, *Industrial Development Survey*, 1974, p. 264.
7. Data available in the FAO *Production Yearbook*, also support this general pattern of substantial growth in total output.
8. Mohamed Abdel Rahman Ali, 'The Propensity to Consume and Economic Development in a Dual Economy: Sudan 1955–67', *Sudan Notes and Records* (Khartoum, 1972), p. 120.
9. Ibid., p. 121.
10. The internal demonstration effect refers to discrepancies in domestic income levels that bring about the desire to attain the associated higher level of consumption. The external demonstration effect refers to international differences in income and consumption levels that tend to raise the level of consumption spending in the lower income country.
11. Hans W. Singer, *International Development: Growth and Change* (New York: McGraw-Hill, 1964), pp. 162–4.
12. While there are no official estimates of the magnitudes of these cash hoardings, discussions with government officials indicate the amounts involved are probably quite large.
13. Mohamed Abdel Rahman Ali, p. 121.
14. The incremental capital-output ratio measures the number of dollars of new investment required to increase output by one dollar.
15. UNIDO, *Summaries of Industrial Development Plans*, Vol. III, 1973, p. 342.

CHAPTER 4

1. This information came from a variety of sources including United Nations, *Yearbook of National Accounts Statistics*; Bank of Sudan, *Annual Reports*; and ILO, *Growth Employment and Equity*, Volume II (1975).
2. Ali Ahmed Suliman, 'Economic Survey', in *African South of the Sahara 1975*, London: Europa Publications, 1975) p. 830. Completion of the Managil-Guneid extensions to the Gezira in the late 1960s brought the land area under gravity irrigation into approximate equality with the land area under pump irrigation. The largest increase in number of schemes and land area brought into pump irrigation came in 1951–60 when almost 910,000 feddans were placed under pump irrigation. Department of Statistics, 'A Report on the Census of Pump Schemes June–August 1963', Vol. 1, Coordinated Picture of Area Irrigated by Pump Schemes in the Republic of the Sudan (Khartoum, Jan 1967 p. 17B).
3. Hamid H. M. Faki and A. M. El Hadari, 'Some Economic Aspects of Wheat Production in the Sudan', *Sudan Journal of Economic and Social Studies*, Summer 1974, pp. 47–8.
4. Ray Vicker, 'Slump in Gum Arabic Output is Ending, Affecting Many Food, Industrial Items', *Wall Street Journal*, 8 Dec, 1975, p. 20. Also El H. M. Awouda, *Production and Supply of Gum Arabic* (Gum Arabic Forest Department, Khartoum, August 1974) pp. 22–3.
5. Sudan Gezira Board, *The Gezira Scheme Past and Present* (Barakat, 1974) p. 9. See also Sudan Gezira Board, *The Gezira Today*, mimeo (no date) pp. 6–7.
6. Arthur Gaitskell, *Gezira: A Story of Development in the Sudan*, Faber & Faber, London, 1959, p. 333.
7. This applies whether fertilizers themselves are imported, or domestic fertiliser production is resorted to. In the period 1961–5 to 1973 consumption of nitrogen fertiliser in the Sudan increased from 22,647 tons in 1961–3 to 45,800 tons in 1971, to 70, 045 tons in 1973 (FAO, *Production Yearbook*, 1973).
8. This project calls for import of 1000 tractors with full equipment, 500 ground-nut harvesters, and 150–200 combine harvesters.
9. With diversification and intensification completed (circa 1980) consumption should rise further to 9 billion cubic metres.
10. These include Rahad I, three sugar plantations, and a kenaf project.
11. Over one-fourth of the total is to be provided by the International Development Association (affiliated with the World Bank), one-fifth by the Kuwait Fund for Economic and Social Development, and the remainder by the US government and other international lenders.
12. Suliman, 'Economic Survey', pp. 830–1.
13. Investment in irrigated acreage in the period 1975–80 calls for completion of Rahad I, sugar plantations, and a kenaf project. In the period 1980–5 irrigated acreage would increase in Rahad II, several sugar plantations, and expansion of pump schemes.
14. ILO, *Growth Employment and Equity*, Volume II (1975, Technical Paper No. 2) p. 15.
15. ILO, *Growth Employment and Equity*, Volume II (Technical Paper No. 3) p. 10.

16. Suliman, 'Economic Survey'. More recent data (1975) released to the authors on an unofficial basis indicate that the livestock population had grown to 14,154 million cattle, 13,373 million sheep, 10,497 goats, and 2698 camels.
17. The herdsman who owns a large number of cattle is given greater recognition, and his opinion is given special weight. This status accrues based on number and not quality of cattle. For this reason many 'culls' and less productive cattle are kept in the herd. Moreover, inbreeding can have undesirable effects on some herds. See A. M. El Hadari, 'Some Socio-Economic Aspects of Farming in the Nuba Mountains, Western Sudan', *Eastern Africa Journal of Rural Development*, 1974, pp. 171–2.
18. Much of the information that follows was obtained from an unpublished (mimeo) report of The Sectoral Committee on Agriculture, East and Central African States, Fifth Meeting, *Forestry Development Sudan*, 1974.
19. The discussion that follows is based on information generously provided by Kamal Khalifa, Director of the Forestry Department during a visit by the authors to the Forestry Headquarters in Khartoum.
20. David Bissouri, 'Development of Forestry Resources of the Southern Region', *Weekly Review*, Sudan News Agency, 23 May, 1975, pp. 18–19.

CHAPTER 5

1. *Area Handbook for the Democratic Republic of the Sudan* (Washington, D.C.: US Government Printing Office, 1973) p. 250.
2. 'Sudan Economic Survey', *African Development*, January 1976, p. S3.
3. The third missing link is the Tan Zam railway link between Zambia and Tanzania.
4. 'Transport: Handmaiden to Trade', *Sudan International*, February 1974, p. 43.
5. Democratic Republic of the Sudan, *Statistical Yearbook 1973*, Table VIII-5.
6. Mustafa Khogali, 'Sudan Transport and the Development of Industry', *Papers Presented to the First Erkowit Conference*, September 1966, Khartoum: Government Printing Press, pp. 162–3.
7. C. Wilkins, *Transport Sector Planning in the Sudan* (Khartoum: National Council for Research–Economic and Social Research Council, September 1974) pp. 4–6.
8. The government has made great efforts to improve statistical data collection on an organised basis, especially since 1970.
9. ADAR Corporation, *The Sudan Transport Study: A Presentation* (Democratic Republic of the Sudan in association with Kuwait Fund for Arab Economic Development, 1974).
10. Hamid Abdel Haleem, 'Power for Industry in the Sudan', in *Papers Presented to the First Erkowit Conference*, 1966, p. 99.
11. This includes the Sudanese Textile factory in North Khartoum, the Shell-BP refinery, the sugar factories at Guneid and Kashm el Girba, and the onion dehydrating factory at Kassala.

12. Faisal B. Imam (editor), *Papers Presented to the First Erkowit Conference*, (University of Khartoum, 1966) p. 3.
13. Ministry of Planning, *Economic Survey 1970* (Democratic Republic of the Sudan, January 1972) p. 27.
14. General Planning and Economic Studies Administration, *Economic Survey 1972*, (Democratic Republic of the Sudan, 1973) pp. 12–13.
15. General Planning and Economic Studies Administration, *Economic Survey 1971*, Democratic Republic of the Sudan, 1973) p. 11.
16. In his study of *Industry in Africa*, A. F. Ewing groups the Sudan among those 'small countries where industrialisation can hardly be said to have started'. This is in contrast to a second group of countries where a range of industry has been initiated, and a third group of countries where there is a significant development of intermediate and capital goods production. Ewing, *Industry in Africa* (Oxford University Press, 1968) pp. 24–5.
17. These plants were among those visited by the authors in 1975.
18. Sayed Abdalla Fadlalla, 'Government Policy Toward Industrialisation', *Papers Presented at the First Erkowit Conference*, 1966, p. 13.
19. Osman Hassan Saeed, *The Industrial Bank of Sudan, 1962–1968: An Experiment in Development Banking* (Khartoum University Press, 1971) p. 54.
20. El-Sayed El-Bushra, 'The Location of Industry in the Sudan', *Papers Presented at the First Erkowit Conference*, 1966, p. 171.
21. In 1966 *per capita* income in the Khartoum area was £S.104.4 per annum, compared with a national average of £S.33.4. Department of Statistics, *Population and Housing Survey 1964–66, Khartoum Province* (September 1968) p. 37; and *Economic Survey 1972*, p. 92.
22. The seven-year development plan (1970–7) states that one priority is the regional distribution of industries throughout the Sudan. However, there is no clear set of incentives that would accomplish this.
23. The original five-year plan (1970–5) was extended two years to coincide with the remaining years of office of President Nimeiri.
24. Democratic Republic of the Sudan, *Interim Report of Action 1971–77*, no date (in Arabic) pp. 8–9.
25. Hikmat Sh. Nashashibi, 'New Lending Techniques by Arab Development Funds', *Euromoney*, Special Supplement on Arab Capital Markets, March 1976, pp. 63–4. According to Mr Nashashibi, Manager of the Kuwait International Investment Company, the Sudan is one of twelve Arab countries that will require financing of a $23 billion combined payments deficit over the period 1976–85. In this connection the main problem is viewed as lack of institutions to appraise project opportunities, rather than lack of funds.
26. Early in 1972 a British-American firm applied for concessions to exploit copper deposits found at Hfrat al Nahas near Port Sudan.
27. Bank of Sudan, *Fourteenth Annual Report*, 1973, pp. 90–1.
28. S. Koncar Kjurdjevic, 'Prospects of Gypsum Industries in the Sudan', *Papers Presented at the First Erkowit Conference*, 1966, p. 322.
29. A. A. R. Elagib, 'Prospects of Utilising Sudan Iron Ores', *Papers Presented at the First Erkowit Conference*, 1966, p. 279.

CHAPTER 6

1. International Monetary Fund, *26th Annual Report on Exchange Restrictions* (1975) p. 437. An effective exchange rate of US$2.50 per Sudanese pound is applied to all exchange transactions other than the purchase of proceeds from exports of cotton and gum arabic, to which the rate of US$2.87 continues to apply. The latter rate results from application of exchange taxes and subsidies of 5.18 piastees per US dollar (15 per cent).
2. The bilateral payments agreement with Czechoslovakia expired at year-end 1974.
3. These changes suggest that the income velocity of M_1 declined from 10 to 5 over the sixteen-year period 1956–72.
4. Five of the seven banks nationalised in 1970 had been foreign-based and foreign-owned. These five and the two domestic banks were nationalised, and shortly after four banks were merged into two successor institutions.
5. 'How the System Works', *Sudan International*, February 1975, p. 7.
6. Bank of Sudan, *Fourteenth Annual Report* (March 1974), p. 60.
7. 'The Banking System in the Sudan', *Sudan International*, February 1975, p. 10.
8. In 1975 the Arab Investment Co. announced a $15.7 million loan to the Kenana Sugar Co. of the Sudan. Fourteen Arab nations are members of the lending institution. *American Banker*, 4 Dec., 1975, p. 10.
9. FAO, *Agricultural Credit in the Near East and the Mediterranean Basin*, Report of the Seminar for Selected Countries of the Near East Region and the Mediterranean Basin held in Rome, Italy, 29 Jan 1973 (United Nations, 1973) pp. 98–9.
10. Ronald I. McKinnon, *Money and Capital in Economic Development* (Brookings Institution, 1973) pp. 68–9.
11. Farah Hassan Adam and William Andrea Apaya, 'Agricultural Credit in the Gezira, *Sudan Notes and Records*, Vol. LIV (1973) p. 112.
12. Ibid., p. 111.
13. Bank of Sudan, *Twelfth Annual Report* (March 1972) p. 73.
14. Bank of Sudan, *Fourteenth Annual Report* (March 1974) pp. 23–9.
15. Bank of Sudan, *Fourteenth Annual Report*, p. 72.
16. Jonathan Levin, 'The Role of Taxation in the Export Economies', in Bird and Oldman, *Readings on Taxation in Developing Countries* (Baltimore: Johns Hopkins, 1964) p. 461.
17. Stanley S. Surrey, 'Tax Administration in Underdeveloped Countries', in Bird and Oldman, *Readings on Taxation in Developing Countries*, pp. 510–11.
18. Sayed M. Nimeiri, 'Commodity Taxation in the Sudan', *Eastern Africa Economic Review*, Nairobi, June 1975, pp. 66–70.
19. Sayed M. Nimeiri, 'Income Elasticity of Tax Structure in the Sudan', *Sudan Journal of Economic and Social Studies* (Khartoum University Press, summer 1974) p. 41.
20. The Thorn study reference is Richard Thorn, 'The Evolution of Public Finances during Economic Development', *Manchester School*, 35 (1967).
21. Nimeiri, *Income Elasticity*, p. 45.
22. Bank of Sudan, *Fourteenth Annual Report*, p. 73.

23. Bank of Sudan, *Twelfth Annual Report*, p. 65.
24. Osman Hassan Saeed, 'Marketability of Securities as an Incentive for Voluntary Savings: A Case Study of the Sudan', *Sudan Notes and Records*, Vol. LII (1971) p. 91.
25. Hugh T. Patrick, 'The Mobilization of Private Gold Holdings, *The Indian Economic Journal*, XI, 2 (1963) pp. 177–83.
26. Saeed, p. 95.

CHAPTER 7

1. Omar Osman and A. A. Suleiman, 'The Economy of the Sudan', in Robson and Lury, *The Economics of Africa* (Allen & Unwin, 1969), pp. 444–5. Mitchell Harwitz ranks the Sudan second among ten African countries in export instability in 'Measuring Export Instability: Theory and African Experience', in S. Schatz, *South of the Sahara: Development in African Economics* (Temple University Press, 1972), p. 285.
2. A detailed account of the foreign exchange control system can be found in the IMF *26th Annual Report on Exchange Restrictions* (1975), pp. 437–9. This analysis is revised and updated each year.
3. Traditionally the Sudanese economy has limped along after the cotton price which produces about 55 per cent of all exports. Inefficient marketing arrangements for cotton resulted in a fall in exports from 1.2 million bales valued at £S.84.3 million in 1973 to 0.5 million bales worth £S.53.2 million in 1974. *Africa Research Bulletin*, Exeter, England, 31 Mar, 1976, p. 3810.
4. Ali Abdalla Ali, 'The Sudan's Invisible Trade, 1956–1969: A Brief Survey', *Sudan Notes and Records*, Vol. LIV (1973), p. 129.
5. Mohamed Abdel Rahman Ali, *Government Expenditure and Economic Development, A Case Study of the Sudan* (Khartoum University Press, 1974), p. 23.
6. Osman and Suleiman, p. 467.
7. Department of Statistics, *Statistical Yearbook 1973* (Democratic Republic of the Sudan), Table IX-4.
8. Mohamed Abdel Rahman Ali, p. 25.
9. Foreign exchange receipts operate as a constraint in connection with the import requirements of real capital formation. A foreign trade gap also may limit capital goods imports.
10. Foreign loans represent gross drawings as included in the balance of payments series published by the central bank, and do not allow for repayments on outstanding foreign loans.
11. World Bank and IDA, *Annual Report*, 1974, pp. 87–8.
12. World Bank and IDA, *Annual Report*, 1975, pp. 56–60.
13. 'A Sudden Interest in Sudan', *The Economist*, 10 May, 1975, p. 103. At this time it was announced that the Arab Fund for Economic and Social Development had just completed a plan projecting a 5.8 per cent yearly growth rate in the Sudan until 1980, and an 8 per cent rate in the period 1980–5. The plan would require an immediate input of $1 billion from Arab fund members and an overall capital inflow of $3 billion to $5 billion over the next ten years.

14. 'Foreign Investment Encouraged', *Sudan International*, Feb 1974, pp. 6–7.
15. In 1975 Triad had developed tentative plans for a $145 million investment in a livestock and cattle project in the vicinity of the Roseires Dam, 300 miles south of Khartoum. The project includes feasibility analysis by the FMC Corporation of California, Triad investment in a new subsidiary, and the use of know-how contributed by the Arizona–Colorado Land and Cattle Co. The project would require transporation facilities including a rail connection at Sennar.

CHAPTER 8

1. Oluwadare Aguda, 'The State and the Economy in the Sudan: From a Political Scientist's Point of View', *Journal of Developing Areas*, Apr 1973, pp. 431–3. The discussion of the next few paragraphs relies heavily on information obtained from this article.
2. An important exception is the agricultural schemes, which have been comparatively successful. Even in these cases greater efficiencies could be obtained. Gezira field inspectors perform work that the tenants could and should carry out. Southern reconstruction has been hampered by bureaucracy and other shortcomings. In 1976 it was reported that only 3.7 million of a total $17.5 million appropriated for southern rehabilitation and reconstruction could be spent. John Darnton, 'In the Lush Southern Sudan Reconstruction is a Slow Process', New York Times, 24 Aug 1976, p. 10.
3. R. F. Wynn, 'The Sudan's 10 Year Plan of Economic Development, 1961/62–1970/71: An Analysis of Achievement', *Journal of Developing Areas*, July 1971, pp. 558–9.
4. Wynn, p. 560. In a study published in 1974 Ahmed H. El Jack and Abdel-Rahman E. A. Taha calculate 592,000 additional manpower required for the plan period in the modern part of the economy. *An Evaluation of Human Resources Planning in the Sudan*, National Council for Research, Khartoum, September 1974, p. 11.
5. Department of Statistics, *Statistical Abstract 1970* (Khartoum), p. 30.
6. World Bank figures suggest that *per capita* real income was unchanged or declined slightly in the Sudan during the decade 1960–70. This reflects diverse trends including little or no change in the large subsistence sector (outlying rural regions), a sharp decline in the southern provinces due to the civil strife, and moderate gains in the urban centres as a result of population shift and a heavier weight of above-average-income-earning family groups. In addition preliminary data from the 1973 population survey referred to in Chapter 2 suggest that population growth in the Sudan was less than previously estimated. This would call for an upward revision in estimates of *per capita* income growth for the decade of the 1960s.
7. Sabi H. Shabtai, 'Army and Economy in Tropical Africa', *Economic Development and Cultural Change*, July 1975, p. 697. Over the period 1964–9 defence and security expenditures represented between 23 per cent and 29 per cent of central government ordinary expenditures in the Sudan. Department of Statistics, *Statistical Abstract 1970*, p. 53.

8. UNIDO, *Summaries of Industrial Development Plans,* Volume III (1973), p. 335.
9. UNIDO, pp. 336–7.
10. These details were published in *Interim Program of Action 1971–77,* no date (in Arabic).
11. The Nile Waters Agreement is due for renewal and renegotiation in 1977.
12. *Interim Program of Action 1971–1977,* p. 6.
13. Aguda, p. 437.
14. Bank of Sudan, *Annual Reports,* 1967–9, Appendix 2.
15. In the period 1960–5 GDP averaged £S.199 million annually.
16. Robin Hallett, *Africa Since 1875* (Ann Arbor: University of Michigan Press, 1974), pp. 181–2.
17. According to Mr Nashashibi, Manager of the Kuwait International Investment Co., the Sudan is one of twelve Arab countries that will require financing of a $23 billion combined payments deficit over the period 1976–85. Himmat Sh. Nashashibi, 'New Lending Techniques by Arab Development Funds', *Euromoney,* Special Supplement on Arab Capital Markets, Mar 1976, pp. 63–4.
18. This question is frequently raised in the literature on promoting economic development. For example, see Michele Guerard, 'Fiscal Versus Trade Incentives for Industrialisation', *Finance and Development* (International Monetary Fund, June 1975), pp. 19–20.
19. Guerard, p. 20.

CHAPTER 9

1. United Nations, *Population Growth and Manpower in the Sudan,* A Joint Study by the United Nations and Government of the Sudan, Population Studies No. 37 (New York, 1964) pp. 1–2.
2. Other manifestations include wide discrepancies in regional income levels, geographic concentration of industry, economic dualism, and an incomplete transportation grid.
3. A. O. Hirschman, *The Strategy of Economic Development* (Yale University Press, 1958) p. 183.
4. World Bank, *Urbanization* (Sector Working Paper, June 1972) pp. 21–4.
5. The re-division of the Sudan accomplished in 1975, whereby new provinces were created, offers promise in this direction.
6. Samba Jack, 'Regional Development in the Context of Overall National Development and Planning', *Economic Bulletin for Africa,* United Nations, Vol. X, No. 2, 1973, p. 34.

Bibliography

PRIMARY SOURCES

ADAR Corporation. *The Sudan Transport Study: A Presentation.* Democratic Republic of the Sudan in association with the Kuwait Fund for Arab Economic Development, 1974.

Bank of Sudan. *Annual Reports.* 1967–1974.

Democratic Repubic of the Sudan.

Census of Population, 1955–56, 1973.

Cotton Public Corporation. *Sudan Cotton, 1975.*

Household Budget Survey for Sudan, 1967–68.

Interim Report of Action, 1971–77.

The Development and Encouragement of Industrial Investment Act, 1974.

Department of Statistics. 'A Report on the Census of Pump Schemes June–August 1963', Vol. 1, *A Coordinated Picture of Area Irrigated by Pump Schemes in the Republic of the Sudan,* 1967.

Department of Statistics. *Population and Housing Survey 1964–66, Blue Nile Province, Urban Areas,* 1968.

Department of Statistics. *Population and Housing Survey 1964–66, Kassala Province, Urban Areas,* 1968.

Department of Statistics. *Population and Housing Survey 1964–66, Kordofan Province, Urban Areas,* 1968.

Department of Statistics. *Population and Housing Survey 1964–66, Northern Province, Urban Areas,* 1968.

General Planning and Economic Studies Administration. *Economic Survey 1971, 1972,* 1973.

Ministry of Agriculture, Food, and Natural Resorces of the Democratic Republic of the Sudan. *Food and the Sudan,* 1974.

Ministry of Agriculture, Forests Department. *Ecological Classification of the Vegetation of the Sudan, 1958.*

Ministry of Foreign Affairs. *Welcome to Sudan,* 1974.

Ministry of Health, Vital and Health Statistics Division. *Annual Statistical Report.* 1972.

Ministry of Industry. *Industrial Survey 1970–71.*

Ministry of Industry and Mining, Government Printer. *Mining and Oil Exploration Laws in the Sudan,* 1974.

Ministry of Planning. *Economic Survey 1970,* January 1972.

Ministry of Planning, Department of Statistics. *Statistical Abstract 1970.*

Ministry of Transport and Communications. *Sudan Telex Directory*, 1975.

National Council for Research. *Employment and Economic Development in the Sudan: A Selected Annotated Bibliography, 1975.*

El Awouda, H. M. Democratic Republic of the Sudan. Gum Arabic Forest Department. *Production and Supply of Gum Arabic, 1974.*

International Bank for Reconstruction and Development. *The Task Ahead for the Cities of the Developing Countries.* Bank Staff Working Paper No. 209, July 1975.

International Labor Office. *Employment, Incomes and Equality: A Strategy for Increasing Productive Employment in Kenya*, Geneva, 1973.

Growth, Employment and Equality. Vols I and II, Technical Papers Nos 2 and 3. Geneva.

Growth, Employment and Equality, A Comprehensive Strategy for Sudan. First Report of the ILO/UNDP employment mission of 1975, Vol. I, October 1975.

International Monetary Fund. *International Financial Statistics.* Washington, D.C.

26th Annual Report on Exchange Restrictions. Washington, D.C., 1975.

O'Brien, J. Democratic Republic of the Sudan. National Council for Research. *The Political Economy of Migrant Labor: A Critique of Conventional Wisdom*, 1974.

Sudan Gezira Board. *The Gezira Today*, 1975.

Information and Publications Section. *The Gezira Scheme Past and Present*, 1974.

Sudan Railway Corporation. *Annual Reports.* 1973–74.

The Sectoral Committee on Agriculture, East and Central African States. *Forestry Development Sudan.* Fifth Meeting, 1974.

United Nations. *Population Growth and Manpower in the Sudan.* A joint study by the United Nations and Government of the Sudan, Population Studies No. 37, 1964.

Survey of Economic Conditions in Africa, 1972. New York, 1974.

Survey of Economic Conditions in Africa, 1973. New York, 1975.

United Nations, Food and Agriculture Organization. *Agricultural Credit in the East and the Mediterranean Basin.* Report of the Seminar for Selected Countries of the Near East Region and the Mediterranean Basin held in Rome, Italy, 29 January 1973.

UNIDO. *Industrial Development Survey.* Special issue for the Second General Conference of UNIDO, Lama, Peru, 12–26 March 1975, New York, 1975.

World Bank. Urbanization. Sector Working Paper, June 1972.

World Bank Atlas. 1974, 1975.

World Bank and IDA. *Annual Reports.* 1971, 1974, 1975.

SECONDARY SOURCES

Abdalla, Abdelgadir Mahmoud. *Studies in Ancient Languages of the Sudan.* Khartoum: Khartoum University Press, 1974.

Albino, Oliver. *The Sudan: A Southern Viewpoint.* Oxford University Press for the Institute of Race Relations, 1970.

Alk, Abbas Ibrahim Muhammad. *The British, the Slave Trade and Slavery in the Sudan 1820–1881.* Khartoum: Khartoum University Press, 1972.

Ali, Mohamed Abdel Rahman. *Government Expenditure and Economic Development, A Case Study of the Sudan.* Khartoum: Khartoum University Press, 1974.

Arkell, A. J. *History of the Sudan.* London: University of London, Athlone Press, 1961.

Barclay, Harold B. *Buurri Al Lamaab: A Suburban Village in the Sudan.* Ithaca: Cornell University Press, 1964.

Beshir, Mohamed O. *The Southern Sudan: Background to Conflict.* Khartoum: Khartoum University Press, 1970.

Day, John R. *Railways of North Africa.* London: Arthur Barker, 1964.

Democratic Republic of the Sudan. *Foreign Trade Statistics 1963 and 1973.*

Department of Statistics. *Statistical Yearbook 1970 and 1973.*

Deng, Francis Mading. *The Dinka of the Sudan.* New York: Holt Rinehart and Winston, 1972.

Tradition and Modernization: *A Challenge for Law Among the Dinka of the Sudan.* Connecticut: Yale University Press, 1971.

El-Bushra, El Sayed, 'The Location of Industry in the Sudan'. Paper presented at the First Erkowit Conference, University of Khartoum, Sudan, September 1966.

El-Jack, Ahmed H. and Abdel-Rahman E. Ali Taha. *An Evaluation of Human Resources Planning in the Sudan 1960–1975.* Khartoum: Khartoum University Press, 1974.

El Mahdi, Saeed M. A. *A Guide to Land Settlement and Registration.* Khartoum: Khartoum University Press, 1971.

Elagib, A. A. R., 'Prospects of Utilizing Sudan Iron Ores'. Paper presented at the First Erkowit Conference, University of Khartoum, Sudan, September 1966.

Ewig, A. E. *Industry in Africa.* London: Oxford University Press, 1968.

Fadlalla, Sayed Abdalla, 'Government Policy Toward Industrialization'. Paper presented at the First Erkowit Conference, University of Khartoum, Sudan, September 1966.

Fitzgerald, Walter. *Africa: A Social, Economic and Political Geography of Its Major Regions.* London: Methuen, 1952.

Gaitskell, Arthur. *Gezira: A Story of Development in the Sudan.* London: Faber & Faber, 1959.

Haleem, Hamid Abdel, 'Power for Industry in the Sudan'. Paper presented at the First Erkowit Conference, University of Khartoum, Sudan, September 1966.

Hallett, Robin. *Africa Since 1875.* Ann Arbor: University of Michigan Press, 1974.

Harrison, Church. *Africa and the Islands.* New York: Wiley, 1964.

Hasan, Yusuf Fadl. *Sudan in Africa.* Khartoum: Khartoum University Press, 1971.

Hassan, Y. F. *The Arabs and the Sudan.* Khartoum: Khartoum University Press, 1963.

Haycock, B. G. 'The Impact of Meroitic and Nubian Civilizations on Africa'. In Yusuf Fadi Hasan, *Sudan in Africa*. Khartoum: Khartoum University Press, 1971.

Henderson, K. K. D. *The Making of the Modern Sudan*. Connecticut: Greenwood Press. 1974.

Hirschman, A. O. *The Strategy of Economic Development*. Connecticut: Yale University Press, 1958.

Holt, P. M. *A Modern History of the Sudan*. New York: Grove Press, 1961.

Imam, Feidal B., ed. *Papers Presented to the First Erkowit Conference*. Khartoum: Khartoum University Press, 1966.

'Sudan Path to Self Sufficiency'. Paper presented to the Second Erkowit Conference, University of Khartoum, Sudan, 1972.

Khogali, Mustafa, 'Sudan Transport and the Development of Industry'. Paper presented at the First Erkowit Conference, University of Khartoum, Sudan, September 1966.

Kjurdjevic, S. Koncar, 'Prospects of Gypsum Industries in the Sudan'. Paper presented at the First Erkowit Conference, University of Khartoum, Sudan, September 1966.

Legum, Colin. *Africa Handbook*. London: Penguin, 1969.

Levin, Jonathan, 'The Role of Taxation in the Export Economies'. In Bird and Oldman, *Readings on Taxation in Developing Countries*. Baltimore: Johns Hopkins, 1964.

Longrugg, S. *The Middle East, A Special Geography*. Chicago: Aldine Publishing Company, 1963.

Mazuri, Ali A. *The Multiple Marginality of the Sudan in Africa*. First International Conference, February, 1968. Khartoum: Khartoum University Press, 1971.

McKinnon, Ronald I. *Money and Capital in Economic Development*. Brookings, 1973.

Mountjoy and Embleton. *Africa: A New Geographical Survey*. New York: Praeger, 1967.

Nelson, Harold, *et al. Area Handbook for the Democratic Republic of the Sudan*. Washington, D.C.: US Government Printing Office, 1973.

Osman, Omar and A. A. Suleiman. 'The Economy of the Sudan'. In Robson and Lury, *The Economies of Africa*. George Allen & Unwin, 1969.

Robinson, E. A. G., ed. *Economic Development for Africa South of the Sahara*. Proceedings of a Conference held by the International Economic Association. New York: St Martin's Press, 1965.

Robson, P. *Economic Integration in Africa*. Northwestern University Press, 1968.

Saeed, Osman Hassan. *The Industrial Bank of Sudan, 1962–1968: An Experiment in Development Banking*. Khartoum: Khartoum University Press, 1971.

Said, Besher Mohammed. *The Sudan: Crossroads of Africa*. Dufour Editions, 1965.

Schatz, S. *South of the Sahara: Development in African Economies*. Temple University Press, 1972.

Shabtai, Sabi H. 'Army and Economy in Tropical Africa'. In *Economic Development and Cultural Change*. 1975.

Suliman, Ali Ahmed. 'Economic Survey'. In *Africa South of the Sahara, 1975.* London: Europa Publications, 1975.

Surrey, Stanley S. 'Tax Administration in Underdeveloped Countries'. In Bird and Oldman, *Readings on Taxation in Developing Countries,* 1964.

Taha, Abdel-Rahman E. Ali. *Labor Relations in the Sudan.* Khartoum: Khartoum University Press, 1975.

United Nations. *Production Yearbook.* 1973.

Yearbook of National Accounts Statistics, 1971–75.

Wai, Dunstan M., ed. *The Southern Sudan.* London: Frank Cass, 1973.

Wilkins, C. *Transport Sector Planning in the Sudan.* National Council for Research – Economic and Social Research Council. Khartoum, 1974.

JOURNALS

Adam, Farah Hassan and William Andrea Apays. 'Agricultural Credit in the Gezira'. *Sudan Notes and Records,* LIV (1973).

Aguda, Oluwadaro. 'The State and the Economy in the Sudan: From a Political Scientist's Point of View'. *Journal of Developing Areas* (Apr 1973).

al Din, Gabal and Mohamed El Awad. 'The Factors Influencing Migration to the Three Towns of the Sudan'. *Sudan Journal of Economic and Social Studies,* Vol. 1, No. 1 (summer 1974).

Ali, Ali Abdalla. 'The Sudan's Invisible Trade, 1956–1969: A Brief Survey'. *Sudan Notes and Records,* LIV (1973).

Bebangambah, J. R. 'Farm Business Planning in Developing Countries: The Need, Problems and Prospects'. *Eastern Africa Journal of Rural Development.* (1975).

Cohen, M. A. 'Cities in Developing Countries: 1975–2000'. *Finance and Development* (Mar 1976).

El Hadari, A. M. 'Some Socio-Economic Aspects of Farming in the Nuba Mountains, Western Sudan'. *Eastern Africa Journal of Rural Development* (1974).

Faki, Hamid H. M. and A. M. El Hadari. 'Some Economic Aspects of Wheat Production in the Sudan'. *Sudan Journal of Economic and Social Studies.* (summer 1974).

Guerard, Michèle. 'Fiscal Versus Trade Incentives for Industrialization'. *Finance and Development,* International Monetary Fund (June 1975).

Hopper, W. David. 'The Development of Agriculture in Developing Countries'. *Scientific American* (Sep 1976).

Ibrahim, Hassan Ahmed. 'The Sudan in the Anglo-Egyption Treaty'. *Sudan Notes and Records,* LIV (1973).

Jack, Samba. 'Regional Development in the Context of Overall National Development and Planning'. *Economic Bulletin for Africa,* United Nations, Vol. X, No. 2 (1973).

Nashashibi, Himmat Sh. 'New Lending Techniques by Arab Development Funds'. *Euromoney,* Special Supplement on Arab Capital Markets (Mar 1976).

Nimeriri, Sayed M. 'Commodity Taxation in the Sudan'. *Eastern Africa Economic Review* (June 1975).

'Income Elasticity of Tax Structure in the Sudan'. *Sudan Journal of Economic and Social Studies* (summer 1974).

No author. 'A Sudden Interest in the Sudan'. *Economist* (May 1975).

'Energy in the Sudan'. *African Development* (Jan 1976).

African Research Bulletin (31 Mar 1976).

American Banker (4 Dec 1975).

'Foreign Investment Encouraged'. *Sudan International* (Feb 1974).

'How the System Works'. *Sudan International* (Feb 1975).

'Sudan Economic Survey'. *African Development* (Jan 1976).

'The Banking System in the Sudan'. *Sudan International* (Feb 1975).

'Transport: Handmaiden to Trade'. *Sudan International* (Feb 1974).

Okereke, O. 'Migrant Labor and its Economic Implication to African Agriculture'. *Eastern Africa Journal of Rural Development* (1975).

Patrick, Hugh T. 'The Mobilization of Private Gold Holdings'. *Indian Economic Journal*, XI, 2 (1963).

Saeed, Osman Hassan. 'Marketability of Securities as an Incentive for Voluntary Savings: A Case Study of the Sudan'. *Sudan Notes and Records*, LII (1971).

Thorn, Richard. 'The Evolution of Public Finances During Economic Development'. *Manchester School*, 35 (1967).

Wynn, R. D. 'The Sudan's Ten Year Plan of Economic Development, 1961/62–1970/71: An Analysis of Achievement'. *Journal of Developing Areas* (July 1971).

Index

For Product Safety Concerns and Information please contact our EU representative GPSR@taylorandfrancis.com Taylor & Francis Verlag GmbH, Kaufingerstraße 24, 80331 München, Germany

Batch number: 10726013

Printed by Printforce, the Netherlands